Uncovering Student Thinking
About **Mathematics**
in the **Common Core**

Grades 3–5

To my sister Stacey for always being there for me.

—Cheryl

*To my husband Sean for his endless support, love,
and belief in me. I am blessed.*

—Emily

Uncovering Student Thinking
About Mathematics
in the Common Core

Grades 3–5

25 Formative Assessment Probes

Cheryl Rose Tobey
Emily R. Fagan

CORWIN
A SAGE Company

CORWIN
A SAGE Company

FOR INFORMATION:

Corwin
A SAGE Company
2455 Teller Road
Thousand Oaks, California 91320
(800) 233-9936
www.corwin.com

SAGE Publications Ltd.
1 Oliver's Yard
55 City Road
London EC1Y 1SP
United Kingdom

SAGE Publications India Pvt. Ltd.
B 1/I 1 Mohan Cooperative Industrial Area
Mathura Road, New Delhi 110 044
India

SAGE Publications Asia-Pacific Pte. Ltd.
3 Church Street
#10-04 Samsung Hub
Singapore 049483

Acquisitions Editor: Jessica Allan
Associate Editor: Kimberly Greenberg
Editorial Assistant: Heidi Arndt
Production Editor: Melanie Birdsall
Copy Editor: Alison Hope
Typesetter: C&M Digitals (P) Ltd.
Proofreader: Jen Grubba
Indexer: Molly Hall
Cover Designer: Anupama Krishnan

Printed in the United States of America

Library of Congress Cataloging-in-Publication Data

Tobey, Cheryl Rose.

Uncovering student thinking about mathematics in the common core, grades 3-5 : 25 formative assessment probes / Cheryl Rose Tobey, Emily R. Fagan.

pages cm
Includes bibliographical references and index.

ISBN 978-1-4522-7024-1 (paperback : acid-free paper)

1. Mathematics—Study and teaching (Elementary)—United States. 2. Educational tests and measurements—United States. 3. Mathematics—Study and teaching (Elementary)—Psychological aspects. 4. Mathematical ability in children—United States—Evaluation. 5. Learning, Psychology of. 6. Effective teaching—United States. I. Fagan, Emily R. II. Title.

QA135.6.T587 2014
372.7'049—dc23   2013029627

This book is printed on acid-free paper.

13 14 15 16 17 10 9 8 7 6 5 4 3 2 1

Contents

Preface

Mathematics Assessment Probes

OVERVIEW

Formative assessment informs instruction and supports learning through a variety of methods and strategies aimed at determining students' prior knowledge of a learning target and using that information to drive instruction that supports each student in moving toward understanding of the learning target. Questioning, observation, and student self-assessment are examples of instructional strategies educators can incorporate to gain insight into student understanding. These instructional strategies become *formative assessment* if the results are used to plan and implement learning activities designed specifically to address the specific needs of the students.

This book focuses on using short sets of diagnostic questions, called Mathematics Assessment Probes (Probes). The Probes are designed to elicit prior understandings and commonly held misunderstandings and misconceptions. This elicitation allows the educator to make sound instructional choices targeted at a specific mathematics concept and responsive to the specific needs of a particular group of students.

> Diagnostic assessment is as important to teaching as a physical exam is to prescribing an appropriate medical regimen. At the outset of any unit of study, certain students are likely to have already mastered some of the skills that the teacher is about to introduce, and others may already understand key concepts. Some students are likely to be deficient in prerequisite skills or harbor misconceptions. Armed with this diagnostic information, a teacher gains greater insight into what to teach. (McTighe & O'Connor, 2005, p. 68)

The Mathematics Assessment Probes provided in this resource are tools that enable teachers in Grades 3 through 5 to gather important insights in a practical way and that provide immediate information for planning purposes.

AUDIENCE

The first collection of Mathematics Assessment Probes and the accompanying Teacher Notes were written for the busy classroom teacher eager for thoughtful, research-based, diagnostic assessments focused on learning difficulties and aimed at enhancing the effectiveness of mathematics instruction. Since the publication of the first three *Uncovering Student Thinking in Mathematics Resources* books (Rose & Arline, 2009; Rose, Minton, & Arline, 2007; Rose Tobey & Minton, 2011), we have continually received requests for additional Probes. Both teachers and education leaders have communicated the need for a collection of research-based Probes that focus on a narrower grade span. In addition to additional Probes for each grade span, educators were eager for an alignment of the Probes to the Common Core Mathematics Standards (Council of Chief State School Officers [CCSSO], 2010). In response to these requests, we set to work writing, piloting, and field testing a more extensive set of Probes for elementary teachers with a focus on targeting mathematics concepts within the new standards. This book is one in a series of *Uncovering* resources for the K–2, 3–5, 6–8, and 9–12 grade spans.

ORGANIZATION

This book is organized to provide readers with an understanding of the purpose, structure, and development of the Mathematics Assessment Probes as well as to support the use of applicable research and instructional strategies in mathematics classrooms.

Chapter 1 provides in-depth information about the process and design of the Mathematics Assessment Probes along with the development of an action-research structure we refer to as a QUEST Cycle. Chapters 2 through 6 contain the collection of Probes categorized by concept strands with accompanying Teacher Notes to provide the specific research and instructional strategies for addressing students' challenges with mathematics. Chapter 7 highlights instructional considerations and images from practice to illuminate how easily and in how many varied ways the Probes can be used in mathematics classrooms. This chapter also highlights how use of the Probes can support students' proficiency with the Common Core's Mathematical Practices.

Acknowledgments

We would like to thank the many mathematics educators who during attendance at various professional development sessions gave valuable feedback about features of the Probes, including structures, concepts to target, and purposes of use.

We especially would like to acknowledge the contributions of the following educators who provided ideas and field-tested Probes, gave feedback on Teacher Notes, scheduled classroom visits, and/or opened their classrooms to us to try Probes or interview students: Amanda Bolanda, Karla Bracy, Jeff Diedrich, Terri Eckes, Emma Fraser, Melissa Guerrette, John Guiron, Tracey Hartnett, Sharon Johnson, Tom Light, Nathan Merrill, Stephanie Pacanza, Nancy Philbrick, Kim Ramharter, Sara Roderick, Bev Schewe, Gal Stetson, Lisa Stevens. Kimberly Tucker, Diane Vang, and Ruth Wilson

Again, we would like to thank our Corwin editor, Jessica Allan, for her continued support and flexibility, and Page Keeley, our science colleague, who designed the process for developing diagnostic assessment Probes and who tirelessly promotes the use of these assessments for formative assessment purposes, helping to disseminate our work in her travels.

We are most grateful for the support, sacrifice, and patience shown by our families, Corey, Grandad, Carly, Jimmy, Bobby, Samantha, and Jack; and Sean, Nellie, and Seamus; throughout the writing of this book.

About the Authors

 **Cheryl Rose Tobey** is a senior mathematics associate at Education Development Center (EDC) in Massachusetts. She is the project director for Formative Assessment in the Mathematics Classroom: Engaging Teachers and Students (FACETS) and a mathematics specialist for Differentiated Professional Development: Building Mathematics Knowledge for Teaching Struggling Students (DPD); both projects are funded by the National Science Foundation (NSF). She also serves as a director of development for an Institute for Educational Science (IES) project, Eliciting Mathematics Misconceptions (EM2). Her work is primarily in the areas of formative assessment and professional development.

Prior to joining EDC, Tobey was the senior program director for mathematics at the Maine Mathematics and Science Alliance (MMSA), where she served as the co–principal investigator of the mathematics section of the NSF-funded Curriculum Topic Study, and principal investigator and project director of two Title IIa state Mathematics and Science Partnership projects. Prior to working on these projects, Tobey was the co–principal investigator and project director for MMSA's NSF-funded Local Systemic Change Initiative, Broadening Educational Access to Mathematics in Maine (BEAMM), and she was a fellow in Cohort 4 of the National Academy for Science and Mathematics Education Leadership. She is the coauthor of six published Corwin books, including three prior books in the *Uncovering Student Thinking* series (2007, 2009, 2011), two *Mathematics Curriculum Topic Study* resources (2006, 2012), and *Mathematics Formative Assessment: 75 Practical Strategies for Linking Assessment, Instruction and Learning* (2011). Before joining MMSA in 2001 to begin working with teachers, Tobey was a high school and middle school mathematics educator for ten years. She received her BS in secondary mathematics education from the University of Maine at Farmington and her MEd from City University in Seattle. She currently lives in Maine with her husband and blended family of five children.

 **Emily R. Fagan** is a senior curriculum design associate at Education Development Center (EDC) in Massachusetts. She has developed print and online curricula as well as professional development and assessment materials in mathematics for twelve years. She was project director of the MathScape Curriculum Center, a project funded by the National Science Foundation (NSF) to support schools, districts, and teachers in curriculum implementation, and she directed the revision of *MathScape: Seeing and Thinking Mathematically* (McGraw-Hill, 2005). She was a developer and facilitator in the Addressing Accessibility in Mathematics Project aimed at supporting struggling learners, particularly those with learning disabilities. Emily currently works on two NSF-funded projects: Differentiated Professional Development: Building Mathematics Knowledge for Teaching Struggling Students (DPD) and Formative Assessment in the Mathematics Classroom: Engaging Teachers and Students (FACETS).

Prior to joining EDC, Emily taught high school and middle school mathematics for nine years in Philadelphia and in Salem and Brookline, Massachusetts. She was a mentor teacher and member of the Massachusetts faculty of the Coalition of Essential Schools. She has long been interested in accessibility in mathematics education and improving opportunities for all students to learn and love math. While mathematics has been her focus for the last two decades, she has also taught science, social studies, and Spanish. Fagan holds an AB cum laude from Harvard University. She lives in Sudbury, Massachusetts, with her husband and their two children.

1

Mathematics Assessment Probes

To differentiate instruction effectively, teachers need diagnostic assessment strategies to gauge their students' prior knowledge and uncover their misunderstandings. By accurately identifying and addressing areas of difficulties, teachers can help their students avoid becoming frustrated and disenchanted with mathematics and can prevent the perception that "some people just aren't good at math." Diagnostic strategies also support instruction that builds on individual students' existing understandings while addressing their identified difficulties. From infancy through prekindergarten, children develop a base of skills, concepts, and misconceptions about numbers and mathematics (National Research Council [NRC], 2005, p. 157). Understanding and targeting these specific areas of difficulty enables teachers to perform focused and effective diagnostic assessment. The Mathematics Assessment Probes in this book allow teachers to target specific areas of difficulty as identified in research on student learning.

The Probes typically include a prompt or question and a series of responses designed specifically to elicit prior understandings and commonly held misunderstandings that may or may not be uncovered during an instructional unit. In the example in Figure 1.1, students are asked to choose from a selection of responses and write about how they determined their answer choice.

This combination of selected responses and further explanation helps to guide teachers in making instructional choices based on the specific needs of their students. Since not all Probes follow the same format, we will discuss the varying formats later in this chapter. If you are wondering what other kinds of Probes are included in this book, take a few moments now to review two or three additional Probes from Chapters 2–6 before continuing reading. But we suggest that you return to read the rest of this chapter before beginning to use the Probes with your students.

At this point, you may be asking; "What is the difference between Mathematics Assessment Probes and other assessments?" Comprehensive

Figure 1.1 Example of a Probe: Decimal Division Estimates

Representing Decimals

Which of the following are equivalent to **0.43**?

	Circle Yes or No:	Explain your answer:
A. **.04 + 0.3**	Yes No	
B.  0.4 0.5	Yes No	
C. 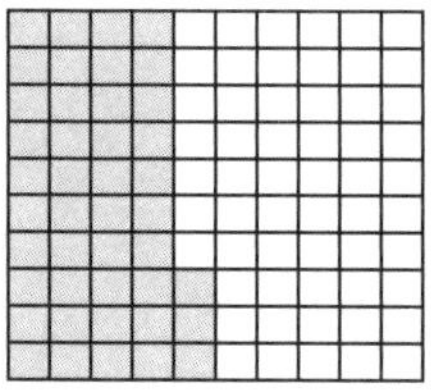 $\square = \dfrac{1}{100}$	Yes No	

diagnostic assessments for mathematics such as AIMSweb (Pearson) and assessments from the Northwest Education Association (NWEA) as well as the many state- and district-developed assessments can provide information important for finding entry points and current levels of understanding within a defined progression of learning for a particular mathematics subdomain such as operations and algebraic thinking. Such assessments will continue to play an important role in schools because they allow teachers to get a snapshot of student understanding across multiple subdomains, often at intervals throughout the year depending on the structure of the assessment.

Consider the following vignette:

> Are you wondering about the Probes? If you are, we suggest reviewing the following Probes as initial examples:
>
> - Rounding Decimals, p. 80
> - Equivalent Fractions Card Sort, p. 102
> - Naming the Perimeter, p. 159

Are They Equivalent?

In an intermediate classroom, the teacher uses a Probe to uncover students' explanations of how to determine equivalent and nonequivalent products and quotients of various two-digit numbers (for example, is 16 × 24 equal to 24 × 16? Is 36 ÷ 12 equal to 12 ÷ 36)? By creating a bar graph of students' responses to anonymously display students' ideas, the teacher and the class can see that many students believe that both products and quotients are equivalent regardless of the order of the numbers. Knowing that this is a common misunderstanding cited in the research literature and seeing that the data from her own class mirror that misunderstanding, the teacher designs a lesson that involves the students in using visual models to model the multiplication and division of various two-digit numbers. After students experience modeling the operations, they revisit their original ideas and have an opportunity to revise them. The next day, students are given the task of defining the commutative property of multiplication. They work in small groups to demonstrate the property and explain why there is no commutative property for division. At the end of the lesson, students are asked to reflect on their original thinking on the Probe about whether the products and quotients were or were not equivalent. (Adapted from Keeley & Rose Tobey, 2011, p. 2)

The Probe used in this vignette, the Are They Equivalent? Probe, serves as a diagnostic assessment at several points during the two-day lesson. The individual elicitation allows the teacher to diagnose students' current understanding; the conversation and practice around modeling the operations both builds the teacher's understanding of what students are thinking and creates a learning experience for students to further develop their understanding of the commutative property. The individual time allotted for reflection allows the teacher to assess whether students are able to integrate this new knowledge with former conceptions or whether additional instruction or intervention is necessary.

Rather than addressing a variety of math concepts, Probes focus on a particular subconcept within a larger mathematical idea. By pinpointing one subconcept, the assessment can be embedded at the lesson level to address conceptions and misconceptions while learning is under way, helping to bridge from diagnostic to formative assessment.

Helping all students build understanding in mathematics is an important and challenging goal. Being aware of student difficulties and the sources of those difficulties, and designing instruction to diminish them, are important steps in achieving this goal (Yetkin, 2003). The process of using a Probe to diagnose student understandings and misunderstandings and then responding with instructional decisions based on the new information is the key to helping students build their mathematical knowledge. Let's take a look at the complete Probe implementation process we call the **QUEST** *Cycle*:

- **Q**uestioning student understanding: Determine the key mathematical understandings you want students to learn.
- **U**ncovering student understanding: Use a Probe to uncover understandings and areas of difficulties.
- **E**xamining connections to research and educational literature: Prepare to answer the question, In what ways do your students' understandings relate to those described in the research base?
- **S**urveying the student responses: Analyze student responses to better understand the various levels of understanding demonstrated in their work.
- **T**eaching implications: Consider and follow through with next steps to move student learning forward.

Figure 1.2   Quest Cycle

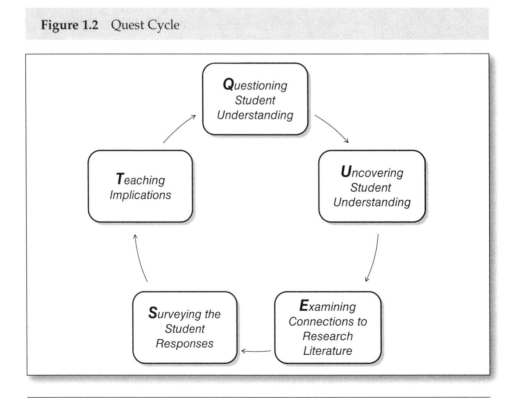

Source: Adapted from Rose, Minton, & Arline (2007).

Note that in the Are They Equivalent? vignette, portions of this cycle are repeated several times within the described instructional period.

The remaining parts of this chapter describe important components of the QUEST Cycle for implementing Probes, including background information on the key mathematics, the structure of the Probes, and connections to the research base. In addition, you will learn about how to get started with administering the Probes.

QUESTIONING STUDENT UNDERSTANDING: DETERMINE THE KEY MATHEMATICAL CONCEPTS YOU WANT STUDENTS TO LEARN

The Common Core State Standards for Mathematics (referred to as the Common Core or CCSSM) define what students should understand and are the basis of the targeted mathematics concepts addressed by the Probes in this book. These understandings include both conceptual knowledge and procedural knowledge, both of which are important for students' mathematical development.

> Research has strongly established that proficiency in subjects such as mathematics requires conceptual understanding. When students understand mathematics, they are able to use their knowledge flexibly. They combine factual knowledge, procedural facility, and conceptual understanding in powerful ways. (National Council of Teachers of Mathematics [NCTM], 2000, p. 20)

Think about the experience of following step-by-step driving directions to an unfamiliar destination using the commands of a GPS but never having viewed a road map of the area. Although it may be easy to follow the directions one step at a time, if you lose your satellite reception, you will likely not know where to turn next or even which direction to head. Using a GPS without a road map is like learning procedures in math without understanding the concepts behind those procedures. Learners who follow the steps of a mathematical procedure, without any conceptual understanding connected to that procedure, may get lost when they make a mistake. Understanding the bigger picture enables learners to reason about a solution and/or reconstruct a procedure.

This relationship between understanding concepts and being proficient with procedures is complex. Table 1.1 provides some examples of each type of understanding for a variety of contexts.

The relationship between understanding concepts and being proficient with procedures is further developed in the examples of the Probes that follow. Both conceptual understanding and procedural flexibility are important goals that complement each other in developing strong mathematical abilities. Each is necessary, and only together do they become sufficient.

Table 1.1 Procedural vs. Conceptual Understanding

Procedural Knowledge	*Accompanying Conceptual Understanding*	*Examples*
Learn and apply a series of steps	• Explain why the steps make sense mathematically. • Use reasoning to rebuild the steps if needed. • Make connections between alternative steps that could be used to find the solution.	Able to describe and connect two different models for adding two fractions such as $\frac{3}{4}$ and $\frac{1}{2}$. Able to interpret a graph to tell about a data set.
Find the answer	• Justify whether the answer makes sense (numerical example: reasoning about the size of numbers and a mathematical operation). • Troubleshoot a mistake. • Represent thinking with symbols, models, and/or diagrams. • Show flexibility in representing mathematical situations.	Able to reason that $10.3 \div 0.2$ must be about 50, since there are five 0.2's in 1 and 5×10 is 50. Able to sort a collection of quadrilaterals based on their characteristics.
Memorize facts	• Generate answer quickly when unable to recall a fact (automaticity).	Has an efficient method to multiply facts not remembered by recall such as 6×9 (6×10, subtract 6) and 3×4 (3×3, add 3).

The following examples of Probes will further distinguish conceptual and procedural understandings.

Example 1: Volume of the Box Probe

Figure 1.3 Volume of the Box

Volume of the Box

Find the volume of each box below.

Circle the correct answer:	Explain your choice:
1. 6 m 3 m 10 m a. 28 m³ b. 180 m³ c. I can't determine the volume.	
2. 30 square meters 4 m a. 34 m³ b. 120 m³ c. I can't determine the volume.	

The Volume of the Box Probe (see Figure 1.3) is designed to elicit whether students understand the volume of a rectangular prism formula numerically and quantitatively (NCTM, 2003, p. 101). Students who correctly determine the volume of the first problem, yet choose "c. Not enough information" for the second problem may be able to apply the volume formula, $V = l \times w \times h$, when given a length, width, and height, but lack the ability to apply the formula to a varied representation of the concept. The following student responses to "Explain Your Reasoning" for item 2 are indicative of conceptual understanding of the formula:

- The first part is just done for you. Thirty square meters is like the $l \times w$ already multiplied. Now times the height to get 120 square meters total.
- This is like when we filled the box with cubes. The first layer is the bottom and then how many layers you need gets multiplied by the number of cubes in the layer. So, 30 in the bottom layer × 4 layers would give you 120 cubes.

More information about this Probe can be found on pages 164–167.

Example 2: Comparing Lengths Probe

Figure 1.4 Comparing Lengths

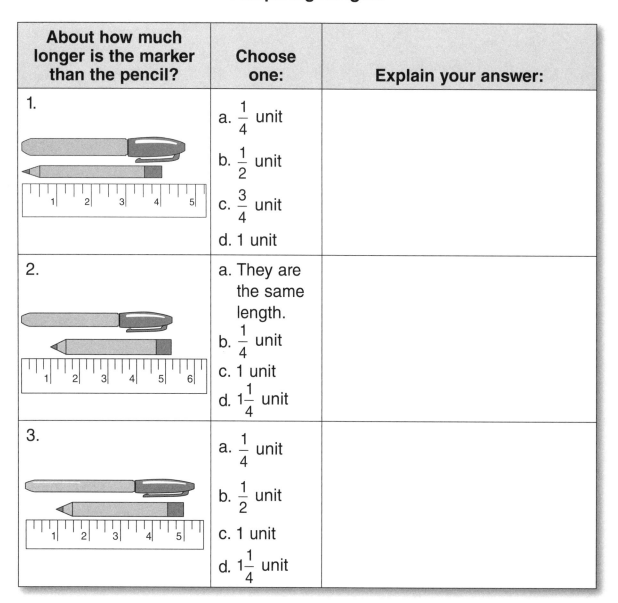

Comparing Lengths

About how much longer is the marker than the pencil?	Choose one:	Explain your answer:
1.	a. $\frac{1}{4}$ unit b. $\frac{1}{2}$ unit c. $\frac{3}{4}$ unit d. 1 unit	
2.	a. They are the same length. b. $\frac{1}{4}$ unit c. 1 unit d. $1\frac{1}{4}$ unit	
3.	a. $\frac{1}{4}$ unit b. $\frac{1}{2}$ unit c. 1 unit d. $1\frac{1}{4}$ unit	

In the Comparing Lengths Probe (see Figure 1.4), students with conceptual and procedural understanding are able to use the ruler to determine the difference in length. Students who have conceptual understanding view length measure as more than just where the end of an object aligns to a labeled hash mark on a ruler and understand that difference in measures is determined by the number of units that one object is longer than the other.

More information about this Probe can be found on pages 135–141.

Example 3: Multiplication and Division Sentences Probe

Figure 1.5   Multiplication and Division Sentences (Number Models)

Multiplication and Division Sentences (Number Models)

1. **Alex went for a walk and saw 4 nests each with 3 eggs.**

What number sentence can be used to find the total number of eggs?

Circle one: Explain why you chose that number sentence:

A. $4 + 3 = ?$

B. $4 + 4 + 4 + 4 = ?$

C. $4 \times 3 = ?$

D. $3 \times 3 \times 3 \times 3 = ?$

2. **Min is making gift bags for her friends. If she puts 3 pencils in each bag and she has 12 pencils in all, how many gift bags can she make?**

What number sentence can be used to find the number of gift bags?

Circle one: Explain why you chose that number sentence:

A. $12 \times 3 = ?$

B. $12 + 3 = ?$

C. $12 \div 3 = ?$

D. $3 \div 12 = ?$

In the Multiplication and Division Sentences Probe (see Figure 1.5), students with conceptual and procedural understanding pay attention to the context of the problems to determine how the numbers should be grouped or divided and the number of those groups or divisions. Rather than focusing solely on key words as a problem–solving approach, these students are able to represent the problem based on an approach that models the situation. Students can solve the problem accurately and can describe how the numbers involved in modeling the problem relate back to the context.

More information about this Probe can be found on pages 35–40.

UNCOVERING STUDENT UNDERSTANDING: USE A PROBE TO UNCOVER UNDERSTANDINGS AND AREAS OF DIFFICULTIES

Misunderstandings are likely to develop as a normal part of learning mathematics. These misunderstandings can be classified as conceptual misunderstandings, overgeneralizations, preconceptions, and partial conceptions. These are summarized in Figure 1.6, and each is described in more detail below.

Figure 1.6 Mathematics Assessment Probes

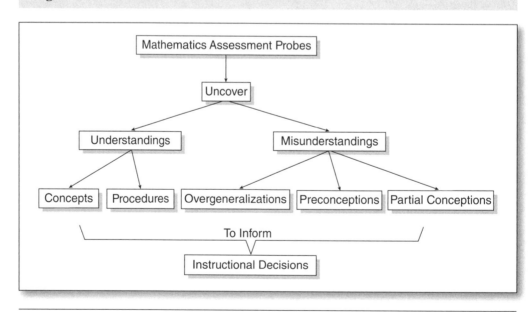

Source: Adapted from Rose, Minton, & Arline (2007).

In *Hispanic and Anglo Students' Misconceptions in Mathematics*, Jose Mestre (1989) summarizes cognitive research as follows: Students do not come to the classroom as "blank slates" (Resnick, 1983). Instead, they come with theories constructed from their everyday experiences. They have actively constructed these theories, an activity crucial to all successful learning. Some of the theories that students use to make sense of the world are, however, incomplete half-truths (Mestre, 1989). They are misconceptions.

Misconceptions are a problem for two reasons. First, when students use them to interpret new experiences, misconceptions interfere with learning. Second, because they have actively constructed them, students are emotionally and intellectually attached to their misconceptions. Even when students recognize that their misconceptions can harm their learning, they are reluctant to let them go. Given this, it is critical that teachers uncover and address their students' misconceptions as early as possible.

For the purposes of this book, misconceptions will be categorized as *preconceptions, overgeneralizations, partial conceptions,* and *conceptual misunderstandings.* The following brief summary describes each of these categories of misconception.

- **Preconceptions:** Ideas students have developed from previous experiences, including everyday interactions and school experiences. Often preconceptions are accurate at the level of mathematics experience but could be an issue if students do not consciously integrate new mathematical ideas.
- **Overgeneralizations:** Information extended or applied to another context in an inappropriate way. Overgeneralizations include vernacular issues related to differences between the everyday meaning of words and their mathematical meaning.
- **Partial Conceptions:** Hybrids of correct and incorrect ideas. This may result from difficulty generalizing or connecting concepts or distinguishing between two concepts.
- **Conceptual Misunderstandings:** Content students "learned" in school but that has been misinterpreted; these misunderstandings often go unnoticed by the teacher. Students often make their own meaning out of what is taught. (Adapted from Keeley, 2012)

Table 1.2 provides an example from each of the above categories. The examples provided are from progressions for the Common Core State Standards in Mathematics written by the Common Core Standards Writing Team (2011a, 2011b, 2011c).

Some misunderstandings do not fall distinctly into one category but can be characterized in more than one way. For example, the conceptual misunderstanding of the equal sign as "the answer is" can also be considered to be an overgeneralization. In addition, some misconceptions are more deeply rooted and difficult to change than others. It is important to make the distinction between what we might call a silly mistake and a more fundamental mistake, one that may be the product of a deep-rooted misunderstanding. In her guest editorial, "Misunderstanding Misconceptions," Page Keeley

Table 1.2 Misconceptions: Categories and Examples

Misconception Category	Example
Preconceptions: Ideas students have from previous experiences, including everyday interactions.	• The decimal point is used to signify the location of the ones place, but its location may suggest there should be a "oneths" place to its right in order to create symmetry with respect to the decimal point. (Common Core Standards Writing Team, 2011a, p. 12)
Overgeneralizations: Extending information to another context in an inappropriate way.	• Students sometimes have difficulty perceiving the unit on a number line diagram. When locating a fraction on a number line diagram, they might use as the unit the entire portion of the number line that is shown on the diagram, for example indicating the number 3 when asked to show $\frac{3}{4}$ on a number line diagram marked from 0 to 4. (Common Core Standards Writing Team, 2011b, p. 3)
Partial Conceptions: Using some correct and some incorrect ideas. This may result from difficulty generalizing or connecting concepts or distinguishing between two concepts.	• Rounding to the unit represented by the leftmost place is typically the sort of estimate that is easiest for students. Rounding to the unit represented by a place in the middle of a number may be more difficult for students (the surrounding digits are sometimes distracting). (Common Core Standards Writing Team, 2011a, p. 11)
Conceptual Misunderstandings: Content that students "learn" in school but have misinterpreted and internalized, which often goes unnoticed by the teacher. Students often make their own meaning out of what is taught.	• Equations with one number on the left and an operation on the right (e.g., 5 = 2 + 3 to record a group of 5 things decomposed as a group of 2 things and a group of 3 things) allow students to understand equations as showing in various ways that the quantities on both sides have the same value (p. 10). Students who only see equations written in one way often misunderstand the meaning of the equal sign and think that the "answer" always needs to be to the right of the equal sign. (Common Core Standards Writing Team, 2011c, p. 10)

Source: Common Core Standards Writing Team (2011a, 2011b, 2011c).

describes various practitioner misunderstandings related to using the science Probes in the National Science Teachers Association's *Uncovering Student Ideas in Science* series (Keeley, 2012). Both in our work with Page and with mathematics educators using the *Uncovering Student Thinking in*

Mathematics resources, we have encountered many similar misunderstandings among teachers:

- *All misconceptions are the same.* The word *misconception* is frequently used to describe all ideas students bring to their learning that are not completely accurate. In contrast, researchers often use labels such as *alternative frameworks, naïve ideas, phenomenological primitives, children's ideas*, etc., to imply that these ideas are not completely "wrong" in a student's common-sense world.

- *Misconceptions are a bad thing.* The word *misconception* seems to have a pejorative connotation to most practitioners. According to constructivist theory, when new ideas are encountered, they are either accepted, rejected, or modified to fit existing conceptions. It is the cognitive dissonance students experience when they realize an existing mental model no longer works for them that makes them willing to give up a preexisting idea in favor of a scientific one. Having ideas to work from, even if they are not completely accurate, leads to deeper understanding when students engage in a conceptual-change process (Watson & Konicek, 1990).

- *All misconceptions are major barriers to learning.* Just as some learning standards have more weight in promoting conceptual learning than others, the same is true of misconceptions. For example, a student may have a misconception for only one type of problem situation (see Figure 1.5, Solving Number Stories) but can make great strides in learning to model and represent operations for other situations. (Adapted from Keeley, 2012.)

To teach in a way that avoids creating any misconceptions is not possible, and we have to accept that students will make some incorrect generalizations that will remain hidden unless the teacher makes specific efforts to uncover them (Askew & Wiliam, 1995). Our job as educators is to minimize the chances of students' harboring misconceptions by knowing the potential difficulties students are likely to encounter, using assessments to elicit misconceptions and implementing instruction designed to build new and accurate mathematical ideas.

The primary purpose of the Probes is to elicit understandings and areas of difficulties related to specific mathematical ideas. In addition to these content-specific related targets, the Probes also elicit skills and processes related to the Mathematical Practices of the Common Core State Standards, especially those related to the use of reasoning and explanation. If you are unfamiliar with these Mathematical Practices or would like a refresher, you can find descriptions of them in Appendix A.

WHAT IS THE STRUCTURE OF A PROBE?

The Probes are designed to include two levels of response, one for elicitation of common understandings and misunderstandings and the other for the elaboration of individual student thinking. Each of the levels is described in more detail below.

Level 1: Answer Response

Since the elicitation level is designed to uncover common understandings and misunderstandings, a structured format using stems, correct answers, and distractors is used to narrow ideas found in the related research. The formats typically fall into one of four categories, shown in Figures 1.7 through 1.10.

Selected Response

- Two or more items are provided, each with one stem (or prompt), one correct answer, and one or more distractors.

Figure 1.7   Comparing to $\frac{1}{2}$

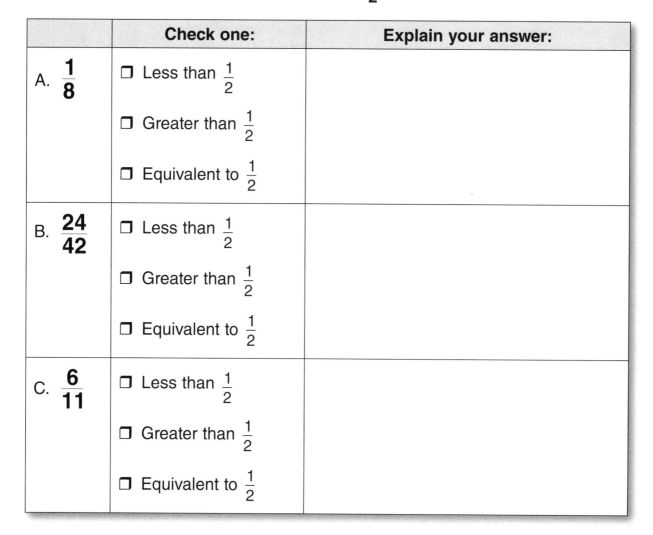

Comparing to $\frac{1}{2}$

	Check one:	Explain your answer:
A. $\frac{1}{8}$	☐ Less than $\frac{1}{2}$ ☐ Greater than $\frac{1}{2}$ ☐ Equivalent to $\frac{1}{2}$	
B. $\frac{24}{42}$	☐ Less than $\frac{1}{2}$ ☐ Greater than $\frac{1}{2}$ ☐ Equivalent to $\frac{1}{2}$	
C. $\frac{6}{11}$	☐ Less than $\frac{1}{2}$ ☐ Greater than $\frac{1}{2}$ ☐ Equivalent to $\frac{1}{2}$	

Math-Talk Probe

- Two or more statements are provided, and students choose the statement they agree with. This format is adapted from *Concept Cartoons in Science Education,* created by Stuart Naylor and Brenda Keogh (2000) for probing student ideas in science.

Figure 1.8 Evaluating Expressions

Evaluating Expressions

Four students are trying to evaluate the expression:

$$10[25 + 2(250 - 47)] + 235$$

They cannot agree on their first step. Read what they think and decide who has the best idea.

Circle one:	Explain your choice:
Andy	
Ben	
Caryn	
Dan	

Choose one person who you think is wrong about where to start. How would you explain to this person why the answer is wrong?

Who?_____

Why?

Examples and Nonexamples Card Sort

- Several examples and nonexamples are given. The teacher cuts out the cards, and students are asked to sort the items into the correct piles.

Figure 1.9   What's the Angle? Cards for Sort

What's the Angle? Cards for Sort

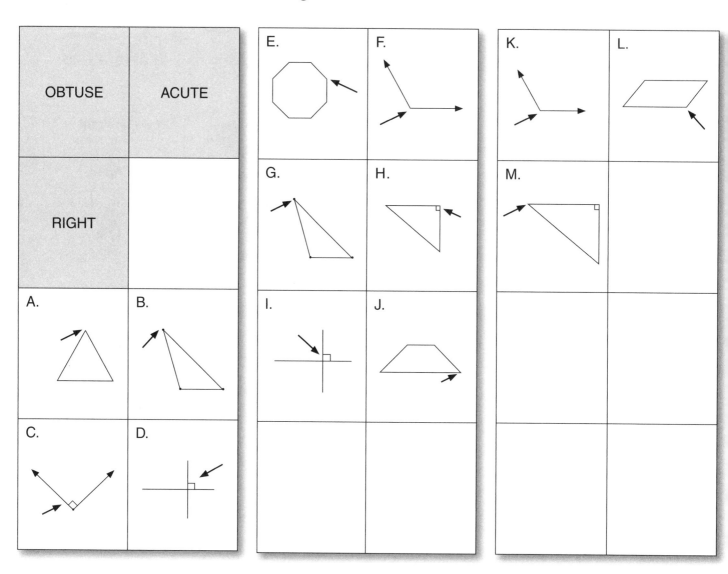

Justified List

- Two or more separate problems or statements are provided, and students must justify each answer they choose as correct.

Figure 1.10 Representing Decimals

Representing Decimals

Which of the following are equivalent to **0.43**?

	Circle Yes or No:	Explain your answer:
A. **.04 + 0.3**	Yes No	
B. (number line with point between 0.4 and 0.5)	Yes No	
C. (grid) $\square = \dfrac{1}{100}$	Yes No	
D. $\dfrac{4}{10} + \dfrac{3}{100}$	Yes No	
E. $\dfrac{4}{3}$	Yes No	
F. **3 tenths and 13 hundredths**	Yes No	

Level 2: Explanation of Response Choice

The second level of each of the Probes is designed so students can elaborate on the reasoning they used to respond to the Level 1 elicitation question. Mathematics teachers gain a wealth of information by delving into the thinking behind students' answers, not just when answers are wrong but also when they are correct (Burns, 2005). Although the Level 1 answers and distractors are designed to target common understandings and misunderstandings, the elaboration level allows educators to look more deeply at student thinking. Often a student chooses a specific response, correct or incorrect, for a typical reason. Also, there are many different ways to approach a problem correctly; therefore, the elaboration level allows educators to look for patterns in thinking and in methods used. Chapter 7 delves more deeply into expectations for this elaboration and its relationship to the Common Core Mathematical Practices (often shortened to Mathematical Practices).

QUEST CYCLE: STRUCTURE OF THE SUPPORTING TEACHER NOTES

The Teacher Notes, included with each Probe, have been designed to help you prepare for a QUEST Cycle. The first two components of the cycle, *determining questions around the key mathematics* and *uncovering student understandings and areas of difficulties,* have been described more fully above. We will use the description of the Teacher Notes to provide more details about the remaining components of the cycle.

Questions to Consider About the Key Mathematical Concepts

This section of the Teacher Notes helps to focus a teacher on the key conceptual and procedural mathematics addressed by the particular Probe and gives information about alignment to Common Core State Standards at a particular grade level. Figure 1.11 shows an example from this section of the Completing Multiplication Sentences Teacher Notes.

Figure 1.11   Questions to Consider About the Key Mathematical Concepts

Do students apply understanding of equality and the operation of multiplication to determine the missing value in an equation? To what extent do they

- think flexibly about equations and the meaning of the equals sign?
- demonstrate an understanding of the operation of multiplication and foundational number concepts related to multiplication?

Common Core Connection (3.OA)

Grade: Third

Domain: Operations and Algebraic Thinking

Clusters:

A. **Represent and solve problems involving multiplication and division.**

3. OA.A.4. Determine the unknown whole number in a multiplication or division equation relating three whole numbers.

B. **Understand properties of multiplication and the relationship between multiplication and division.**

3. OA.B.5. Apply properties of operations as strategies to multiply and divide.

Uncovering Student Understanding About the Key Concepts

This section of the Teacher Notes (Figure 1.12) breaks down the concepts and ideas described in the "Questioning" section into specific understandings and areas of difficulty targeted by the Probe.

Figure 1.12   Uncovering Student Understanding About the Key Concepts

Using the Completing Multiplication Sentences Probe can provide the following information about how students are thinking about equality and the meaning of the equal sign.

Do they

- correctly interpret aspects of the equation, such as
  - the factors?
  - the equal sign?
  - the box symbol representing the missing value?

OR

Do they

- multiply quantities without consideration of all of the numbers and meanings of the symbols contained in the equation?

- apply an understanding of the equal sign as a symbol of equality that tells them the quantities on each side have the same value?

OR

- interpret the equal sign as a "stop sign" that means "when you reach the equal sign, it's time to compute"?

Exploring Excerpts From Educational Resources and Related Research

This section of the Teacher Notes (Figure 1.13) includes excerpts from cognitive research and other educational resources that address common areas of difficulty targeted by the Probe. The excerpts are meant to provide some background from the research base behind the development of the Probe. The references provide an opportunity for you to seek additional information when needed. This research base is an important component in the Probe development process. More information on the origin of the Probe development process can be found in Appendix B.

Figure 1.13 Exploring Excerpts From Educational Resources and Related Research

---

Common areas of difficulty for students:

The equal sign is one of the most important symbols in elementary arithmetic, in algebra, and all mathematics using numbers and operations. At the same time, research dating from 1975 to the present indicates that "=" is a very poorly understood symbol. . . . Students' experiences lead them to believe that one side of the equal sign—usually the left side—is the problem and the other side is the answer. Their understanding of = is more like the button on the calculator—it is what you press to get the answer. It separates the problem from the answer. (Van de Walle, 2007, p. 260)

Knowing different methods of computation will be of little value to students if they do not understand what each operation does. As our students solve problems in the world around them, they must understand the *meaning* [italics in original] of each operation if they are to know which operations to compute and which numbers to use within a problem situation. . . . Without such "deep meanings" for the operations, students tend to merely react to the symbols they see and do not make the needed connections conceptually. For example, the student who sees 56 + □ = 83 may think "56 and 83"; it is *plus* [italics in original] so you add the numbers. . . . Later, students encounter comparable situations involving multiplication and division. (Ashlock, 2006, pp. 53–54)

Surveying the Prompts and Selected Responses in the Probe

This section of the Teacher Notes (Figure 1.14) includes information about the prompt, selected response/answer(s), and distractors. Example student responses are given for a selected number of elicited understandings and misunderstandings. This initial preparation will help expedite the analysis process once you administer the Probe to students.

Figure 1.14 Surveying the Prompts and Selected Responses in the Probe

There are four selected response items, each with four choices. The items are designed to elicit understandings and common difficulties as described below.

If a student chooses	It is likely that the student
1. 4 2. 9 3. 2 4. 2 (correct responses)	• understands the structure of the equation and the meaning of the equal sign as a symbol of equivalence, and is able to apply multiplication facts to solve the problem [See Sample Student Response 1]. *Look for indication of the student's understanding in the written explanations of how the student got the answer.*
1. 36 2. 18 3. 20 4. 30	• multiplies the terms on the opposite side of the equation from the missing number box, ignoring the third or fourth term [See Sample Student Response 2].
1. 3 2. 6 3. 4	• mirrors the number on the opposite side of the equal sign [See Sample Student Response 3].
3. 10 4. 15	• multiplies the terms on the same side of the equal sign as the unknown number [See Sample Student Response 4].

*T*eaching Implications and Considerations

Being aware of student difficulties and their sources is important, but acting on that information to design and provide instruction that will diminish those difficulties is even more important. The information in this section of the Teacher Notes (Figure 1.15) is broken into two categories: (1) ideas for eliciting more information from students about their understanding and difficulties, and (2) ideas for planning instruction in response to what you learned from the results of administering the Probe. Although these ideas are included in the Teacher Notes, we strongly encourage you to pursue additional research-based teaching implications.

Figure 1.15 Teaching Implications and Considerations

Ideas for eliciting more information from students about their understanding and difficulties:

• For students who appear to treat the equal sign as a signal to stop and compute or those who mirror the number on the opposite side of the equal sign, ask questions directed at learning more about their understanding of the equal sign and equations:

   ○ What does the equal sign mean to you? (Is the student thinking about the equal sign only as "the answer is coming"?)

   ○ What does this blank box in the equation mean to you?

   ○ Can you read this equation out loud to me?

   ○ How does this equation look the same or different from others that you have seen?

(Continued)

(Continued)

- To learn about how the student approached answering the problems, ask
  - "What did you do to decide on an answer choice?"
  - "Why did you multiply these two numbers? What about this other number?"
  - "Can you multiply these numbers using a model?"

Ideas for planning instruction in response to what you learned from the results of administering the Probe:

- During instruction, use explicit language, such as "is the same as" and "is equivalent to" to refer to the equal sign as a relationship between the two numbers and/or expressions on opposite sides of the symbol.
- Connect and contrast the equal sign to symbols of inequality to build understanding of equality.
- Use visual models that support the idea of equivalence (e.g., balance, seesaw).
- Provide opportunities for students to make connections from symbolic notation to the representation of an equation.
- Vary the way that you show multiplication and division equations, using different numbers of terms on each side of the equal sign to avoid students developing only one image of what an equation should look like.
- Explore equations as either true or false to build understanding of the equal sign. (e.g., "Is this equation true or false? 8 + 7 = 5 + 9"), and ask students to explain their reasoning.
- Use interactive technology to have students model equivalence.

Included in the Teaching section of the Teacher Notes are sample student responses; examples of these are shown in Figure 1.16.

Figure 1.16 Sample Student Responses to Division Estimates

Responses That Suggest Understanding

Sample Student Response 1

Student circled 4 on Problem 1 and wrote, "Both have to multiply to same number. Because 3 × 12 is 3 × 10 plus 3 × 2. So we have to find the number × 9 that is 36. This is why I circled 4."

Responses That Suggest Difficulty

Sample Student Response 2

Student circled 18 on Problem 2 and wrote, "3 × 6 is 18 so that's the right answer."

Sample Student Response 3

Student circled 4 on Problem 3 and wrote, " = is the same so 4 is 4."

Sample Student Response 4

Student circled 15 on Problem 4 and wrote, "6 × 5 = 30 and 5 × 3 = 15."

Variations

For some Probes, adaptations and variations are provided and can be found following the Teacher Notes and sample student responses to the Probe. A variation of a Probe provides an alternative structure (selected response, multiple selections, opposing views, or examples/nonexamples) for the question within the same grade span. In contrast, an adaptation to a Probe is similar in content to the original, but the level of mathematics is changed for a different grade span.

Action Research Reflection Template

A Reflection Template is included in Appendix C. The Reflection Template provides a structured approach to working through the QUEST Cycle with a Probe. The components of the template are described in Figure 1.17.

Figure 1.17 Reflection Template

Questions to Consider About the Key Mathematical Concepts

What is the concept you wish to target? Is the concept at grade level or is it a prerequisite?

Uncovering Student Understanding About the Key Concepts

How will you collect information from students (e.g., paper pencil, interview, student response system, etc.)? What form will you use (e.g., one-page Probe, card sort, etc.)? Are there adaptations you plan to make? Review the summary of typical student responses.

Exploring Excerpts From Educational Resources and Related Research

Review the quotes from research about common difficulties related to the Probe. What do you predict to be common understandings and/or misunderstandings for your students?

Surveying the Prompts and Selected Responses in the Probe

Sort by selected responses then re-sort by trends in thinking. What common understandings/misunderstandings did the Probe elicit? How do these elicited understandings/misunderstandings compare to those listed in the Teacher Notes?

Teaching Implications and Considerations

Review the bulleted list and decide how you will take action. What actions did you take? How did you assess the impact of those actions? What are your next steps?

BEGINNING TO USE THE PROBES

Now that you have a background on the design of the Probes, the accompanying Teacher Notes, and the QUEST Cycle, it is time to think about how to get started using the Probes with your students.

Choosing a Probe: Determining which Probe to use depends on a number of factors, including time of year, alignment to curriculum, and range of abilities within your classroom. We recommend you spend some time reviewing the Probes at your grade level first but also that you make note of additional Probes that may be appropriate for your students.

Deciding How to Administer a Probe: Depending on your purpose, Probes can be given to one student or to all students in your classroom. You may wish to give a Probe to only one student (or several) if you notice the student or group is struggling with a related concept. By giving a Probe to all students, you can gain a sense of patterns of understanding and difficulty in order to target instruction. Although all Probes can be given as a written explanation, we encourage you to use the Probes as interview prompts in order to learn even more about your students' thinking. Using the Probes in interviews is described in more detail in Chapter 7.

Talking With Students About Probes: Probes are not meant to be graded! We have found that students are very much able to understand the diagnostic nature of the Probes, especially if the process is shared explicitly with them. Talk to your students about the importance of explaining their thinking in mathematics and why you will ask additional questions to understand more about their thinking.

When giving a Probe, be sure to read through the directions out loud, repeating them as necessary. Do not try to correct students on the spot; instead, ask additional probing questions to determine whether the additional questions prompt the student to think differently. If not, do not stop to try to teach the students "in the moment." Instead, take in the information and think about the next appropriate instructional steps. If students are having difficulty, reassure them that you will be working with them to learn more about the content in the Probe.

HOW TO NAVIGATE THE BOOK

This chapter provided the background information needed to begin to dig into the Probes and think about how you will use them with your students. The next five chapters include twenty-five sets of Probes and accompanying Teacher Notes, and the final chapter includes additional considerations for using the Probes.

Chapters 2 Through 6: The Probes

Table 1.3 provides an "at-a-glance" look at the targeted grade span and related domain of the content of the twenty-five Probes.

Table 1.3 Mathematics Assessment Probes

Chapter	Page Numbers	Probe	CCSS (Common Core State Standards) Domain
Grade 3			
2	29	Completing Number Sentences	Operations and Algebraic Thinking
2	35	Multiplication and Division Sentences (Number Models)	Operations and Algebraic Thinking
3	62	Rounding Whole Numbers	Number and Operations: Base Ten
3	68	Subtracting Whole Numbers	Number and Operations: Base Ten
4	98	Locating a Fraction on a Number Line	Number and Operations: Fractions
4	102	Equivalent Fractions Card Sort	Number and Operations: Fractions
5	130	What Does the Graph Say?	Measurement and Data
5	135	Comparing Lengths	Measurement and Data
6	154	Finding Area	Geometric Measurement
Grade 4			
2	41	Classifying Numbers Card Sort	Operations and Algebraic Thinking
2	49	Which Answer Makes Sense? (Working With Remainders)	Operations and Algebraic Thinking
3	73	Are They Equivalent?	Number and Operations: Base Ten
4	110	Representing Decimals	Number and Operations: Fractions
4	116	Comparing to $\frac{1}{2}$	Number and Operations: Fractions
4	122	Fraction Estimates: Addition	Number and Operations: Fractions
6	159	Naming the Perimeter	Measurement and Data
6	168	Classifying Angles Card Sort	Geometry
Grade 5			
2	54	Evaluating Expressions	Operations and Algebraic Thinking
3	80	Rounding Decimals	Number and Operations: Base Ten
3	85	Adding Decimals	Number and Operations: Base Ten
3	91	Decimal Division Estimates	Number and Operations: Base Ten
5	142	Estimating Measures	Number and Operations: Fractions
5	148	Comparing Metric Measures	Measurement and Data
6	164	Volume of the Box	Geometric Measurement
6	178	Names of the Shape	Geometry

The beginning of each Probe chapter (Chapters 2–6) includes background on the development of the Probes to align with the relevant Common Core domain and standards and a summary chart to guide your review and selection of Probes and variations to use with your students.

Chapter 7: Additional Considerations

The QUEST Cycle components are explained in detail within this chapter as well as for each specific Probe through the accompanying Teacher Notes. In addition to these ideas that are "specific to the Probe" are instructional considerations that cut across the Probes. Such considerations include ways to use the Probes over time to promote mathematical discussions, support and assess students' ability to provide justification, and promote conceptual change.

We recommend that you scan the contents of Chapter 7 before beginning to use the Probes but that you not try "do it all" the first time out. After using the Probes, return to Chapter 7 to pinpoint one or two considerations to implement and try out those ideas before returning to consider implementing additional ideas.

FINAL CHAPTER 1 THOUGHTS

We hope these Probes will support you in your work in trying to uncover your students' thinking and understanding and will inspire you to explore ways to respond to their strengths and difficulties in order to move students' learning forward.

2

Operations and Algebraic Thinking Probes

The content of the Probes in this chapter aligns with the standards for Grades 3 through 5. The Probes and their variations will also be relevant beyond the aligned grade level for students in higher grades who have not yet met standards from previous grade levels as well as for students who have already met the standards at their own grade level.

We developed these Probes to address the following critical areas of focus, described in the standards (CCSS0, 2010):

- Understand properties of multiplication and the relationship between multiplication and division.
- Represent and solve problems involving multiplication and division.
- Solve problems involving the four operations, and identify and explain patterns in arithmetic.
- Gain familiarity with factors and multiples.
- Generate and analyze patterns and relations.
- Write and interpret numerical expressions.

> The content of the Probes in this chapter aligns with the standards for Grades 3 through 5. The Probes and their variations will also be relevant beyond the aligned grade level for students in higher grades who have not yet met standards from previous grade levels as well as for students who have already met the standards at their own grade level.

The standards and their related questions, as well as the Probes associated with them, are shown in the following table.

Common Core Math Content

Common Core Mathematical Content	Related Question	Probe Name
Determine the unknown whole number in a multiplication or division equation relating three whole numbers. 3.OA.A.4 Apply properties of operations as strategies to multiply and divide. 3.OA.B.5	Do students apply understanding of equality and the operation of multiplication to determine the missing value in an equation?	Completing Number Sentences (p. 29) Variation: Completing Number Sentences: Addition (p. 34)
Use multiplication and division within 100 to solve word problems in situations involving equal groups, arrays, and measurement quantities. 3.OA.A.3	When solving problems involving equal groups and measurement quantities, can students make sense of the sequence of actions in the problem to determine an appropriate number model?	Multiplication and Division Sentences (Number Models) (p. 35)
Gain familiarity with factors and multiples. Determine whether a given whole number in the range 1–100 is prime or composite. 4.OA.B.4	Can students classify a number as prime or composite?	Classifying Numbers Card Sort (p. 41) Variation: Prime or Composite? (p. 48)
Solve multistep word problems posed with whole numbers and having whole-number answers using the four operations, including problems in which remainders must be interpreted 4.OA.A.3	Do students understand that how a remainder is used depends on the context of the problem being answered?	Which Answer Makes Sense? (Working With Remainders) (p. 49)
Use parentheses, brackets, or braces in numerical expressions and evaluate expressions with these symbols. 5.OA.A.1	Do students understand how to interpret mathematical symbols and apply order of operations to simplify expressions?	Evaluating Expressions (p. 54) Variation: Order of Operations (p. 59)

Take a look at the variations that are available with some of the Probes in this chapter. All of these variations address operations and algebraic thinking but may extend the idea or offer a different structure for administering them. When available, variation Probes follow the Teacher Notes and associated reproducibles for the related original Probe.

Completing Number Sentences

1. $$9 \times \square = 3 \times 12$$ Circle the number that belongs in the box: **3 4 27 36**	Write about how you got your answer.
2. $$3 \times 6 = \square \times 2$$ Circle the number that belongs in the box: **6 9 12 18**	Write about how you got your answer.
3. $$5 \times 4 = \square \times 5 \times 2$$ Circle the number that belongs in the box: **2 4 10 20**	Write about how you got your answer.
4. $$6 \times 5 = 5 \times 3 \times \square$$ Circle the number that belongs in the box: **2 15 25 30**	Write about how you got your answer.

Teacher Notes: Completing Number Sentences

Questions to Consider About the Key Mathematical Concepts

Do students apply understanding of equality and the operation of multiplication to determine the missing value in an equation? To what extent do they

- think flexibly about equations and the meaning of the equals sign?
- demonstrate an understanding of the operation of multiplication and foundational number concepts related to multiplication?

Common Core Connection (3.OA)

Grade: Third

Domain: Operations and Algebraic Thinking

Clusters:

A. Represent and solve problems involving multiplication and division.

3.OA.A.4. Determine the unknown whole number in a multiplication or division equation relating three whole numbers.

B. Understand properties of multiplication and the relationship between multiplication and division.

3.OA.B.5. Apply properties of operations as strategies to multiply and divide.

Uncovering Student Understanding About the Key Concepts

Using the Completing Multiplication Sentences Probe can provide the following information about how students are thinking about equality and the meaning of the equal sign.

Do they

- correctly interpret aspects of the equation, such as
  - the factors?
  - the equal sign?
  - the box symbol representing the missing value?

OR

Do they

- multiply quantities without consideration of all of the numbers and meanings of the symbols contained in the equation?

Do they

- apply an understanding of the equal sign as a symbol of equality that tells them the quantities on each side have the same value?

OR

Do they

- interpret the equal sign as a "stop sign" that means "when you reach the equal sign, it's time to compute"?

Exploring Excerpts From Educational Resources and Related Research

Common areas of difficulty for students:

The equal sign is one of the most important symbols in elementary arithmetic, in algebra, and all mathematics using numbers and operations. At the same time, research dating from 1975 to the present indicates that "=" is a very poorly understood symbol. . . . Students' experiences lead them to believe that one side of the equal sign—usually the left side—is the problem and the other side is the answer. Their understanding of = is more like the button on the calculator—it is what you press to get the answer. It separates the problem from the answer. (Van de Walle, 2007, p. 260)

Knowing different methods of computation will be of little value to students if they do not understand what each operation does. As our students solve problems in the world around them, they must understand the *meaning* [italics in original] of each operation if they are to know which operations to compute and which numbers to use within a problem situation. . . . Without such "deep meanings" for the operations, students tend to merely react to the symbols they see and do not make the needed connections conceptually. For example, the student who sees 56 + □ = 83 may think "56 and 83"; it is *plus* [italics in original] so you add the numbers. . . . Later, students encounter comparable situations involving multiplication and division. (Ashlock, 2006, pp. 53–54)

Surveying the Prompts and Selected Responses in the Probe

There are four selected response items, each with four choices. The items are designed to elicit understandings and common difficulties as described in the following table:

If a student chooses	It is likely that the student
1. 4 2. 9 3. 2 4. 2 (correct responses)	• understands the structure of the equation and the meaning of the equal sign as a symbol of equivalence, and is able to apply multiplication facts to solve the problem [See Sample Student Response 1]. *Look for indication of the student's understanding in the written explanations of how the student got the answer.*
1. 36 2. 18 3. 20 4. 30	• multiplies the terms on the opposite side of the equation from the missing number box, ignoring the third or fourth term [See Sample Student Response 2].
1. 3 2. 6 3. 4	• mirrors the number on the opposite side of the equal sign [See Sample Student Response 3].
3. 10 4. 15	• multiplies the terms on the same side of the equal sign as the unknown number [See Sample Student Response 4].

Teaching Implications and Considerations

Ideas for eliciting more information from students about their understanding and difficulties:

- For students who appear to treat the equal sign as a signal to stop and compute or those who mirror the number on the opposite side of the equal sign, ask questions directed at learning more about their understanding of the equal sign and equations:
  - What does the equal sign mean to you? (Is the student thinking about the equal sign only as "the answer is coming"?)
  - What does this blank box in the equation mean to you?
  - Can you read this equation out loud to me?
  - How does this equation look the same or different from others that you have seen?

- To learn about how the student approached answering the problems, ask
  - "What did you do to decide on an answer choice?"
  - "Why did you multiply these two numbers? What about this other number?"
  - "Can you multiply these numbers using a model?"

Ideas for planning instruction in response to what you learned from the results of administering the Probe:

- During instruction, use explicit language, such as "is the same as" and "is equivalent to," to refer to the equal sign as a relationship between the two numbers and/or expressions on opposite sides of the symbol.

- Connect and contrast the equal sign to symbols of inequality to build understanding of equality.
- Use visual models that support the idea of equivalence (e.g., balance, seesaw).
- Provide opportunities for students to make connections from symbolic notation to the representation of an equation.
- Vary the way that you show multiplication and division equations, using different numbers of terms on each side of the equal sign to avoid students developing only one image of what an equation should look like.
- Explore equations as either true or false to build understanding of the equal sign. (e.g., "Is this equation true or false? $8 + 7 = 5 + 9$"), and ask students to explain their reasoning.
- Use interactive technology to have students model equivalence.

Sample Student Responses to Completing Number Sentences

Responses That Suggest Understanding

Sample Student Response 1

Student circled 4 on Problem 1 and wrote, "Both have to multiply to same number. Because 3×12 is 3×10 plus 3×2 or $30 + 6$. So we have to find the number $\times 9$ that is 36. This is why I circled 4."

Responses That Suggest Difficulty

Sample Student Response 2

Student circled 18 on Problem 2 and wrote, "3×6 is 18 so that's the right answer."

Sample Student Response 3

Student circled 4 on Problem 3 and wrote, " = is the same so 4 is 4."

Sample Student Response 4

Student circled 15 on Problem 4 and wrote, "$6 \times 5 = 30$ and $5 \times 3 = 15$."

Variation: Completing Number Sentences: Addition

1. $3 + 3 = \boxed{} + 5$ Circle the number that belongs in the box: **6** **11** **1**	Write about how you got your answer.
2. $8 + 3 = 7 + \boxed{}$ Circle the number that belongs in the box: **11** **4** **18**	Write about how you got your answer.
3. $6 + \boxed{} = 8 + 7$ Circle the number that belongs in the box: **21** **9** **2**	Write about how you got your answer.
4. $3 + 5 = \boxed{} + 4$ Circle the number that belongs in the box: **4** **8** **12**	Write about how you got your answer.

Multiplication and Division Sentences (Number Models)

1. **Alex went for a walk and saw 4 nests, each with 3 eggs.**

What number sentence can be used to find the total number of eggs?

Circle one: Explain how you chose that number sentence:

A. 4 + 3 = ?

B. 4 + 4 + 4 + 4 = ?

C. 4 × 3 = ?

D. 3 × 3 × 3 × 3 = ?

2. **Min is making gift bags for her friends. If she puts 3 pencils in each bag and she has 12 pencils in all, how many gift bags can she make?**

What number sentence can be used to find the number of gift bags?

Circle one: Explain how you chose that number sentence:

A. 12 × 3 = ?

B. 12 + 3 = ?

C. 12 ÷ 3 = ?

D. 3 ÷ 12 = ?

3. **Eli has a scarf that is 40 inches long. Eli's scarf is 2 times longer than Ami's scarf.**

What number sentence can be used to find the length of Ami's scarf?

Circle one: Explain how you chose that number sentence:

A. $2 \times ? = 40$

B. $2 \times 40 = ?$

C. $2 \div 40 = ?$

D. $2 + ? = 40$

---

4. **Diego is lining up baseballs for hitting practice. If he arranges 24 baseballs in 3 equal rows, how many baseballs are in each row?**

What number sentence can Alex use to find the number of baseballs in each row?

Circle one: Explain how you chose that number sentence:

A. $24 \times 3 = ?$

B. $24 - ? = 3$

C. $24 \div ? = 3$

D. $3 \div 24 = ?$

Teacher Notes: Multiplication and Division Sentences (Number Models)

Questions to Consider About the Key Mathematical Concepts

When solving problems involving equal groups and measurement quantities, can students make sense of the sequence of actions in the problem to determine an appropriate number model? To what extent do they

- make sense of the sequence of actions within a problem context to determine whether to multiply or divide the given numbers?
- model the situation with a number sentence or equation that matches their solution process?
- describe how their model and solution relate back to the context?

Common Core Connection (3.OA)

Grade: Third

Domain: Operations and Algebraic Thinking

Clusters:

A. Represent and solve problems involving multiplication and division.

3.OA.A.3. Use multiplication and division within 100 to solve word problems in situations involving equal groups, arrays, and measurement quantities.

Uncovering Student Understanding About the Key Concepts

Using the Multiplication and Division Sentences Probe can provide the following information about how the students are thinking about equal grouping and measurement quantities problem types.

Do they
- recognize equal grouping problems in which the quantities should be grouped OR or divided and the number of those groups or divisions?
- determine the correct number sentence that models the OR problem?

Do they
- choose sentences with corresponding numbers but incorrect operations?

- choose sentences with the correct operation but incorrect order?

Exploring Excerpts From Educational Resources and Related Research

Common areas of difficulty for students:

As with addition and subtraction, each multiplication or division situation involves three quantities, each of which can be the unknown (unknown product, group size unknown, number of groups unknown). The focus of third grade is on Equal Groups of Objects and Arrays of Objects with all three unknowns. Row and column language can be difficult. Array problems are of the simplest form in which a row is a group and Equal Groups language is used ("with 6 apples in each row"). Such problems are a good transition between the Equal Groups and array situations and can support the generalization of the commutative property. (Common Core Standards Writing Team, 2011c, pp. 23–24)

[Recognition of multiplicative problem structure is essential to problem solving.] Experiences solving problems that vary in context and construction are necessary for problem schema acquisition and skill transfer. (Xin, 2008, p. 528)

These transfers [mentioned in Xin excerpt above] do not occur intuitively, they must be explicitly taught by focusing on increasing students' awareness of the connections between new and familiar situations. (Fuchs et al., 2003, p. 293)

Data from the Mathematics Assessment for Learning and Teaching (MaLT) project data base indicate that students have difficulty selecting the correct operation for multiplicative situations. These difficulties include selecting multiplication symbols for division problems or selecting division sign but incorrect order of the quantities involved. (Ryan & Williams, 2007, p. 189)

Surveying the Prompts and Selected Responses in the Probe

The Probe consists of four separate selected response items, each involving an equal grouping or measurement quantity problem. The prompts and selected responses are designed to elicit understandings and common difficulties as described below.

If a student chooses	It is likely that the student
1. C 2. C 3. A 4. C (correct responses)	• is able to makes sense of the sequence of actions in the problem and is able to determine the correct number model [See Sample Student Response 1]. *Look for indication of the student's understanding in the written explanations of how the student got the answer.*

If a student chooses	It is likely that the student
1. A 2. C 3. D 4. B	• does not understand equal grouping or division problem types and is instead choosing addition or subtraction sentences not representative of the multiplicative structure needed [See Sample Student Response 2].
2. D 3. D	• chooses a sentence with an incorrect number order; this choice may indicate an inability to translate between equivalent multiplication and division sentences [See Sample Student Response 3 and 4].

Teaching Implications and Considerations

Ideas for eliciting more information from students about their understanding and difficulties:

- For students who have selected the correct responses but whose explanations are not clear or complete, ask them to explain why their answer makes sense for the problem. Listen for reasoning about how they determined which number sentence models the problem.
- For students who have selected an incorrect answer, ask them to explain what they understand about the context of the problem.
    - What is the answer to this number sentence? How do you know? Why does this answer make sense as an answer to the problem?
    - Can you describe this problem in your own words?
    - Can you create a picture that shows what's happening in this problem?
    - Can you make an estimate of the solution to the problem? Does your number sentence choice give an answer close to your estimate?

Ideas for planning instruction in response to what you learned from the results of administering the Probe:

- Provide opportunities for students to understand the meaning of multiplication and division by investigating situations involving the relationship between equivalent parts and the total amount. (Ashlock, 2006, p. 53)
- Use contexts to explore and model situations involving multiplication and division.
- Have students create their own story problems for each of the problem types: unknown product ($4 \times 3 = ?$), group size unknown ($12 \div 3 = ?$ or $4 \times ? = 12$), and number of groups unknown ($12 \div 4 = ?$ or $? \times 3 = 12$).
- "In developing meaning of operations, ensure that students repeatedly encounter situations in which the same numbers appear in different contexts." (NCTM, 2000, p. 83)

- "When the teacher models representations of number sentences, these representations should reflect the variability students show. In all mathematical problem solving, what matters is the explanation a student gives to relate a representation to a context, and not the representation separated from its context." (Common Core Standards Writing Team, 2011c, p. 13)

Sample Student Responses to Multiplication and Division Sentences (Number Models)

Responses That Suggest Understanding

Sample Student Response 1

The student chose "A" on Problem 3 and wrote, "I want 40 divide by 2 but it is not in the list. Can switch it around to say 2 × something? = 40."

Responses That Suggest Difficulty

Sample Student Response 2

Student chose "B. 24 – ? = 3" for Problem 4 and wrote, "Because he doesn't know how many are in each row."

Sample Student Response 3

Student chose "D. 3 ÷ 12 = ?" for Problem 2 and wrote, "3 pencils divided by 12 is how many bags Min can make."

Sample Student Response 4

Student chose "A. 12 × 3 = ?" for Problem 2 and wrote, "12 groups of 3 is 12 × 3."

Classifying Numbers Card Sort

(Reproducible student cards follow Teacher Notes on p. 46)

Composite	Prime
18	11
72	33
97	2
42	59

57	19
91	25
79	229

Advance Preparation: Create cards by photocopying and cutting out the eighteen cards. Separate the three blank cards and the two label cards from the deck and shuffle the thirteen cards with numbers.

Instructions:

1. Invite the students to sort the cards into two piles: **Prime** and **Composite**. Use the label cards to identify the piles.

2. As students finish the sort, give them the blank cards and ask them to create their own prime and composite cards.

3. Either choose three cards for the students or ask them to choose three cards from the Prime pile. Ask them to explain or show how they knew these cards should go in the Prime pile.

4. Either choose three cards for the students or ask them to choose three cards from the Composite pile. Ask them to explain or show how they knew these cards should go in the Composite pile. Use the recording sheet as appropriate.

Teacher Notes: Classifying Numbers Card Sort

Questions to Consider About the Key Mathematical Concepts

Can students classify a number as prime or composite? To what extent, do they

- apply understanding of multiplication to determine the factors of a number?
- use reasoning and strategies such as divisibility to determine whether a number is prime or composite?

Common Core Connection (4.OA)

Grade: Fourth

Domain: Operations and Algebraic Thinking

Cluster:

B. Gain familiarity with factors and multiples.

4.OA.B.4. Find all factor pairs for a whole number in the range 1–100. Recognize that a whole number is a multiple of each of its factors. Determine whether a given whole number in the range 1–100 is a multiple of a given one-digit number. Determine whether a given whole number in the range 1–100 is prime or composite.

Uncovering Student Understanding About the Key Concepts

Using the Classifying Numbers Card Sort Probe can provide the following information about how students are thinking about prime and composite numbers.

Do they

- correctly apply the definitions of prime (a whole number greater than 1 with only 2 factors, 1 and itself) and composite (a whole number with 3 or more factors)?

OR

Do they

- interchange the definitions or apply an incorrect definition?

- use multiplication facts to determine a number's factors?

- misapply multiplication facts?

Do they		*Do they*
• realize that 2 is a prime number and the only even prime number?	OR	• think all even numbers are composite?
• understand that some odd numbers have more than two factors and are not prime?	OR	• mistakenly think odd numbers are prime or that the words *odd* and *prime* are synonymous?

*E*xploring Excerpts From Educational Resources and Related Research

Common areas of difficulty for students:

Many teachers use factor trees to explore the concept of *prime decomposition* or the breakdown of a number into its prime factors. The factor-tree method is not an ideal way to teach prime decomposition because no tools are used and little emphasis is placed on conceptual understanding. To view decomposition more comprehensively, teachers must move beyond factor trees. [Researchers recommend the use of prime factor tiles as a tool.] (Kurz & Garcia, 2012, p. 52)

In a study of pre-service teachers' understanding of prime and composite numbers, the data showed that many teachers did not see a relationship between prime and composite numbers. In a question asking about the relationship between prime and composite numbers, researchers expected that teachers would mention the idea of prime factorization more frequently than they did. Instead, the research indicates that for some teachers the relationship between prime and composite numbers is simply that they are members of disjoint sets. (Zazkis & Liljedahl, 2004, pp. 183–184)

Some mathematical words are related, but students may confuse their distinct meaning. Examples: factor and multiple; hundred and hundredths; numerator and denominator. . . . Factors and multiples both relate to multiplication and are difficult for students to distinguish between. Mnemonic devices can be created from the etymologies: "Just as factories make products, so do factors make products" and "Every number has a multitude of multiples." (Rubenstein & Thompson, 2006, pp. 108, 111)

*S*urveying the Prompts and Selected Responses in the Probe

The Probe consists of sixteen cards (seven prime, seven composite, and two blank). The prime numbers included in the set of cards are 2, 11, 19,

59, 79, 97 and 229; the composite numbers included in the set are 18, 25, 33, 42, 57, 72, and 91. There are cards with the labels "composite" and "prime" for designating the two piles. The selected numbers are designed to elicit understandings and common difficulties as described below.

If a student	It is likely that the student
Categorizes all numbers correctly (as indicated above)	• is applying correct definitions of prime and composite [See Sample Student Response 1]. *Look for indication of the student's understanding in the written explanations of how the student got the answer.*
Puts a prime number in the composite pile	• does not yet understand the meaning of prime number. • thinks all even numbers are composite. (2, though even, is a prime number) [See Sample Student Response 2]. • has made a factoring or multiplication error.
Puts a composite number in the prime pile	• does not yet understand what it means for a number to be composite. • thinks that odd numbers are prime [See Sample Student Response 2]. • has made a factoring or multiplication error. • has overlooked a pair of factors [See Sample Student Response 3].

Teaching Implications and Considerations

Ideas for eliciting more information from students about their understanding and difficulties:

- Can you explain how you decided which pile to place a number in?
- Do you know what it means for a number to be prime or composite?
- Can you write down all the factors of each number? How might this help you place the number?
- Were some of these cards more difficult for you to place than others? Which ones?
- Are there any cards that you are not feeling sure about? Any that you feel really confident about?
- What is the relationship between prime and composite numbers? How are they similar/different?

Ideas for planning instruction in response to what you learned from the results of administering the Probe:

- Use concrete objects such as beans, coins, or counters to model factors. The number 9 can be modeled with one group of nine objects or three groups of three objects, so it is a composite. Prime numbers can only be modeled in one way.

- Use concrete materials such as prime factor tiles (tiles with prime numbers written on them) to build the concept of decomposition and enable manipulation that static illustrations such as factor trees don't allow.
- Use visual representations to build understanding of factors—for example, have students draw rectangles on grid paper to show that the dimensions represent each of two factors and the area represents the number. Help them see that prime numbers can only be represented by one rectangle while composite numbers can be represented by more than one rectangle.
- Discuss characteristics of numbers and make predictions about the number of factors they have.
- Use factor trees, prime factorization, or other systems of organization to help students keep track of the factors, but only after students have a conceptual understanding of factoring.
- Explore divisibility rules as one way to determine whether a number is prime or composite (e.g., numbers that end in a 0 are divisible by 10, 5, and 2, so any number other than 0 that ends in 0 is composite).
- Define prime number in a way that supports students in building understanding of the concept and helps them make connections between composite numbers and prime factorization. For example, use statements such as "prime numbers have exactly 2 factors" and avoid negative definitions like "prime numbers cannot be factored" or "prime numbers are only divisible by 1."

Sample Student Responses to Classifying Numbers Card Sort

Responses That Suggest Understanding

Sample Student Response 1

Student categorized all correctly, and wrote for one explanation, "2 is prime even though it is even. Only 2 × 1 or 1 × 2 is 2. Nothing else works."

Responses That Suggest Difficulty

Sample Student Response 2

Student categorized all odds as prime, and wrote for one explanation, "91 is prime because not all numbers are paired up, there is one left over. 45 and 45 and 1."

Sample Student Response 3

Student categorized 57 as prime, and wrote for explanation, "prime because only 57 × 1. I tried other numbers but couldn't find ones that × to 57. Tried 3 and 7."

Classifying Numbers Cards

Composite	Prime
18	11
72	33
97	2
42	59

57	19
91	25
79	229

Variation: Prime or Composite?

Determine if the number is prime or composite and explain your choice.

	Circle one:	Explain your choice:
A. **49**	Prime Composite	
B. **2**	Prime Composite	
C. **59**	Prime Composite	
D. **21**	Prime Composite	
E. **11**	Prime Composite	

Which Answer Makes Sense? (Working With Remainders)

---

1. Diana has 27 new photos to add to her photo album. She can fit 6 photos on a page. How many pages does she need in order to add all of her new photos?

Which number of pages best represents this situation?

Circle one: Explain your choice:

A. 4   D. 21

B. 4.5   E. 32

C. 5

---

2. Shanice has some string licorice to share with her friends. She has a string that is 57 inches long, and she wants to share it equally among 6 friends. How much should she give to each friend?

Which number of inches best represents this situation?

Circle one: Explain your choice:

A. 9   D. 51

B. 9.5   E. 63

C. 10

---

3. Mrs. Mathews has 48 pencils to give to her students. She wants to share the pencils evenly among her 15 students so that each student gets the same number of pencils, and she gives away as many pencils as possible. How many pencils should Mrs. Mathews give to each student?

Which number of pencils best represents this situation?

Circle one: Explain your choice:

A. 3   D. 40

B. 3.2   E. 60

C. 4

Teacher Notes: Which Answer Makes Sense? (Working With Remainders)

Questions to Consider About the Key Mathematical Concepts

Do students understand that how a remainder is used depends on the context of the problem being answered? To what extent, do they

- demonstrate an understanding of whether or not to round an answer and, when rounding, whether to round up or down?
- explain their approach to solving a word problem and reasoning for interpreting the remainder?

Common Core Connection (4.OA)

Grade: Fourth

Domain: Operations and Algebraic Thinking

Cluster:

A. Use the four operations with whole number to solve problems.

4.OA.A.3. Solve multistep word problems posed with whole numbers and having whole-number answers using the four operations, including problems in which remainders must be interpreted. Represent these problems using equations with a letter standing for the unknown quantity. Assess the reasonableness of answers using mental computation and estimation strategies including rounding.

Uncovering Student Understanding About the Key Concepts

Using the Which Answer Makes Sense? Probe can provide the following information about how students are thinking about how to interpret the remainder of division story problems.

Do they

- apply contextual information from the problem to determine how best to represent the solution?

OR

- explain their reasoning and approach to solving the problem and selecting a response?

OR

Do they

- give the answer in a format that does not make sense for the problem context?
- always rely on one method of rounding?

- have difficulty explaining their reasoning?

Exploring Excerpts From Educational Resources and Related Research

Common areas of difficulty for students:

Addressing what to do with remainders must be central to teaching about division. In fact, one of the most common errors students make on high-stakes assessments is to divide and then not pay attention to the context when selecting their response. (Van de Walle, Karp, & Bay-Williams, 2013, p. 161)

Common Learning Pitfall: Thinking division only pertains to whole numbers with a whole-number quotient. Some students do not recognize division situations when the numbers are not whole and are not clearly divisible by one another. (Bay Area Mathematics Task Force, 1999, p. 52)

Surveying the Prompts and Selected Responses in the Probe

The Probe consists of three word problems, each with five selected responses. The prompts and selected responses are designed to elicit understandings and common difficulties as described below.

If a student chooses	It is likely that the student
1. C 2. B 3. A (correct responses)	• is able to interpret the remainders in the context of the word problem. In problems one and three, the answer must be rounded. The photos will take up seven and a half pages, so Diana needs to round up to eight pages. It doesn't make sense to give part of a pencil to a student, so Mrs. Mathews must round down (or off) to three pencils to give to each of her students the same number and she'll need to keep the ten leftover pencils. Licorice can be partitioned into parts of an inch, so this solution should be given as an exact measure rather than rounded up or down [See Sample Student Response 1]. *Look for indication of the student's understanding in the written explanations of how the student got the answer.*
1. B 3. B	• has correctly computed for the context but has not interpreted the remainder correctly. The answer should be rounded to make sense given the context [See Sample Student Response 2].

(Continued)

(Continued)

If a student chooses	It is likely that the student
1. A 2. A or C 3. C	• has not interpreted the remainder correctly. While the student may have calculated correctly, the student has rounded incorrectly [See Sample Student Response 3].
1. D or E 2. D or E 3. D or E	• has not interpreted the word problem correctly and has performed addition or subtraction rather than division [See Sample Student Response 4].

Teaching Implications and Considerations

Ideas for eliciting more information from students about their understanding and difficulties:

- For students who have selected the correct responses but whose explanations are not clear or complete, ask them to explain why their answer makes sense for the problem. Listen for reasoning about how they calculated and why they rounded or did not round their answer.
- For students who have selected an incorrect answer, ask them to explain what they understand about the context of the problem.

  o Can you tell me a little about what is going on in this problem?
  o What calculation did you make to solve this problem?
  o Can you explain how you decided which of these three answers to choose (the rounded and not rounded answer)?

Ideas for planning instruction in response to what you learned from the results of administering the Probe:

- Help students learn that when a situation is out of context, there are two ways to express a remainder mathematically: as a quantity left over, or as a fraction or decimal of the divisor. In real-life situations, though, there are additional ways to handle the remainder: rounding up to the next whole number regardless of the size of the remainder, rounding to the nearest whole number, or disregarding the remainder and expressing only the whole number (rounding off).
- Use concrete materials and drawings to help students model and make sense of problem-solving contexts and decide which treatment of the remainder makes sense for the context.
- Focus on building conceptual understanding of division using problems whose solutions do not include remainders. Introduce remainders when students have a foundation of division and sequence problems so that the remainder concept can be first explored with friendlier remainders.

- Ask students to estimate the answer to story problems before computing. Estimation practice can help build understanding of computational procedures and can help students determine whether their computed answer is reasonable.
- Provide opportunities for students to write story problems requiring the various interpretations of remainders.

Sample Student Responses to Which Answer Makes Sense? (Working With Remainders)

Responses That Suggest Understanding

Sample Student Response 1

Student chose "B" on Problem 2 and wrote, "You give part of the string to the friends. 57 shared by 6 is 9 inches with 3 inches left over. 3 inches shared by the 6 friends is a small amount $\frac{1}{2}$ inch for each. So in all the friends get a piece that is 9 and the other piece that is $\frac{1}{2}$."

Responses That Suggest Difficulty

Sample Student Response 2

Student chose "B" on Problem 3 and wrote, "I divided. A remainder means a decimal so B is only one with a decimal."

Sample Student Response 3

Student chose "A" on Problem 1 and wrote, "27 divided by 6 is 4. So she can't put 3 of the pictures in the album."

Sample Student Response 4

Student chose "E" on Problem 3 and wrote, "She added more pictures 27 + 6 = 32."

Evaluating Expressions

Four students are trying to evaluate the expression

10[25 + 2(250 − 47)] + 235

They can't agree on their first step. Read what they think and decide who has the best idea.

I think we should start with 10 × 25.

Andy

I think we should do 250 − 47 first.

Ben

I think we should start with 25 and add 2.

Caryn

I don't think it matters where we start.

Dan

Circle one:	Explain your choice:
Andy	
Ben	
Caryn	
Dan	

Choose one person who you think is wrong about where to start. How would you explain to this person why the answer is wrong?

Who?_____

Why?

Teacher Notes: Evaluating Expressions

Questions to Consider About the Key Mathematical Concepts

Do students understand how to interpret mathematical symbols and apply order of operations to simplify expressions? To what extent, do they

- determine which step to take first in evaluating the expression?
- offer an explanation that reflects understanding of the order of operations?

Common Core Connection (5.OA)

Grade: Fifth

Domain: Operations and Algebraic Thinking

Cluster:

A. Write and interpret numerical expressions.

5.OA.A.1. Use parentheses, brackets, or braces in numerical expressions and evaluate expressions with these symbols.

Uncovering Student Understanding About the Key Concepts

Using the Evaluating Expressions Probe can provide the following information about how students are able to apply the mathematical convention of order of operations including interpreting parentheses and brackets.

Do they

- know that there is one correct answer to this problem and that the correct answer depends on the procedure one uses and the order in which the computation is performed?

OR

- know to begin with the innermost grouping symbol (250–247)?

OR

Do they

- think the same answer will result regardless of the order in which the calculations are made?

- compute from left to right?

Do they

- understand that grouping symbols are used to "override" the standard order of operations?

OR

Do they

- ignore the importance of the grouping symbols?

Exploring Excerpts From Educational Resources and Related Research

Common areas of difficulty for students:

The phrase "Please excuse my dear Aunt Sally" or more simply, "PEMDAS" is sometimes used to help students remember the order of operations. Although these mnemonics are helpful, they may lead students to think that addition is done before subtraction and multiplication comes before division. (Van de Walle et al., 2013, p. 473)

Students continue to do poorly on order of operations items on high-stakes assessments, and this is due to a lack of understanding. While part of the order of operations is due to convention (e.g., working from left to right), it is largely due to the meaning of the operations. Because multiplication represents repeated addition, it must be figured first before adding on more. (Van de Walle et al., pp. 473–474)

Surveying the Prompts and Selected Responses in the Probe

The Evaluating Expressions Probe has four agree–disagree prompts related to student thinking about the first step in evaluating a numeric expression. The examples of student thinking are designed to elicit understandings and common difficulties as described below.

If a student chooses	*It is likely that the student*
Ben (correct answer)	• recognizes that the order of operations requires that the expression contained within parentheses nested in the bracket be simplified first [See Sample Student Response 1]. *Look for indication of the student's understanding in the written explanations of how the student got the answer.*

If a student chooses	It is likely that the student
Andy	• computes from left to right without regard to grouping symbols [See Sample Student Response 2].
Caryn	• computes within the brackets from left to right and may or may not know how to interpret the 10 outside the bracket [See Sample Student Response 3].
Dan	• does not understand that expressions must be simplified according to a consistent and universal procedure: the order of operations [See Sample Student Response 4].

Teaching Implications and Considerations

Ideas for eliciting more information from students about their understanding and difficulties:

- Does it matter where you start when you try to simplify this expression? Why?
- What do these symbols mean (bracket, parentheses, 10 outside a bracket)?
- Do you know what the second step in evaluating this expression should be? What about the third step?

Ideas for planning instruction in response to what you learned from the results of administering the Probe:

- To build understanding of grouping and operation symbols and the order of operations, ask students to write a story problem that matches a given expression.
- Use visual display of PEMDAS that arranges the procedure in rows to avoid the common pitfall of thinking that multiplication is performed before division, and addition is performed before subtraction.

    P = parentheses

    E = exponents

    MD = multiplication and division (whichever is first from left to right)

    AS = addition and subtraction (whichever is first from left to right) (Van de Walle et al., 2013, p. 473)

- Have students make up their own variation of the mnemonic "PEMDAS."

- Build understanding that all grouping symbols are performed first. Grouping symbols include *parentheses* ( ), *brackets* [ ], *braces* { }, the *vinculum*—(informally called the *fraction bar*) and the *radical* √ (commonly called the square root symbol). Some recommend using GEMDAS (Graciously, excuse my dear Aunt Sally), not PEMDAS.
- Provide opportunities for students to develop story problems that require the use of grouping symbols.

Sample Student Responses to Evaluating Expressions

Responses That Suggest Understanding

Sample Student Response 1

Student chose "Ben," and wrote, "Ben has the best idea. You should always figure out the equation in the ( ) first. If I started with 25 + 2 I would be missing a step."

Responses That Suggest Difficulty

Sample Student Response 2

Student chose "Andy," and wrote, "Multiplication always comes first."

Sample Student Response 3

Student chose "Caryn," and wrote, "I think Caryn because that is the first problem I see in the equation."

Sample Student Response 4

Student chose "Dan," and wrote, "I think all of them would work because all of them might matter what one you pick because they all work."

Variation: Order of Operations

Three students are trying to evaluate the expression

$$46 - 30 \div 2 \times 3 + 6$$

Which solution do you think is correct?

46 − 30 ÷ 2 × 3 + 6	46 − 30 ÷ 2 × 3 + 6	46 − 30 ÷ 2 × 3 + 6
16 ÷ 2 × 3 + 6	46 − 30 ÷ 6 + 6	46 − 15 × 3 + 6
8 × 3 + 6	46 − 5 + 6	46 − 45 + 6
24 + 6	41 + 6	1 + 6
30	47	7

Andy   *Ben*   *Caryn*

Circle one:	**Explain your choice:**
Andy **Ben** **Caryn**	

Choose one person who you think is wrong about where to start. How would you explain to this person why the answer is wrong?

Who?_____

Why?

3

Number and Operations: Base-Ten Probes

The content of the Probes in this chapter aligns with the standards for Grades 3 through 5. The Probes and their variations will also be relevant beyond the aligned grade level for students in higher grades who have not yet met standards from previous grade levels, as well as for students who have already met the standards at their own grade level.

We developed these Probes to address the following critical areas of focus, described in the standards (CCSS, 2010):

The content of the Probes in this chapter aligns with the standards for Grades 3 through 5. The Probes and their variations will also be relevant beyond the aligned grade level for students in higher grades who have not yet met standards from previous grade levels, as well as for students who have already met the standards at their own grade level.

- Understand the place value system.
- Generalize place value understanding for multi-digit whole numbers.
- Use place value understanding and properties of operations to perform operations with multi-digit whole numbers and with decimals to hundredths.

The standards and their related questions, as well as the Probes associated with them, are shown in the following table.

Remember to take a look at the variations that are available with some of the Probes in this chapter. All of these variations address number and operations in base ten but may extend

Common Core Math Content

Common Core Mathematical Content	Related Question	Probe Name
Use place value understanding to round whole numbers to the nearest 10 or 100. 3.NBT.A.1	Do students understand how to round whole numbers to a given place value?	Rounding Whole Numbers (p. 62)
Fluently add and subtract within 1,000 using strategies and algorithms based on place value, properties of operations, and/or the relationship between addition and subtraction. 3.NBT.A.2	Do students understand subtraction based on place value and/or reasoning about the relationship between addition and subtraction?	Subtracting Whole Numbers (p. 68)
Multiply a whole number of up to four digits by a one-digit whole number, and multiply two two-digit numbers, using strategies based on place value and the properties of operations. 4.NBT.B.5	Do students understand how ideas of whole number decomposition and commutativity can be used to evaluate whether or not multiplication expressions are equivalent?	Are They Equivalent? (p. 73) Variation: Are They Equivalent? (p. 78)
Use place value understanding to round decimals to any place. 5.NBT.A.4	Do students understand rounding decimals as a way of estimating numbers in which you increase or decrease the value of the number to a given place?	Rounding Decimals (p. 80)
Add, subtract, multiply, and divide decimals to hundredths, using concrete models or drawings and strategies based on place value, properties of operations, and/or the relationship between addition and subtraction. 5.NBT.B.7	Do students apply an understanding of place value when adding decimals?	Adding Decimals (p. 85) Variation: Subtracting Decimals (p. 90)
Add, subtract, multiply, and divide decimals to hundredths, using concrete models or drawings and strategies based on place value, properties of operations, and/or the relationship between addition and subtraction. 5.NBT.B.7	When solving problems involving the division of decimal fractions, can students reason about the size of the numbers and the effect of the operation in order to determine a reasonable estimate?	Decimal Division Estimates (p. 91) Variation: Division Estimates (p. 95)

the idea or offer a different structure for administering them. When available, variation Probes follow the Teacher Notes and associated reproducibles for the related original Probe.

Rounding Whole Numbers

Circle the correct answer.	Explain your choice.
1. **Round 199 to the nearest 10** a. 190 b. 200 c. 209 d. 299	
2. **Round 439 to the nearest 100** a. 400 b. 430 c. 440 d. 500	
3. **Round 2,346 to the nearest 10** a. 2,000 b. 2,300 c. 2,340 d. 2,350	

Circle the correct answer.	Explain your choice.
4. **Round 8,199 to the nearest 100** a. 8,000 b. 8,190 c. 8,200 d. 8,209	
5. **Round 24,738 to the nearest 100** a. 24,700 b. 24,708 c. 24,800 d. 25,000	
6. **Round 9,835 to the nearest 10** a. 9,830 b. 10,000 c. 9,800 d. 9,840	

Teacher Notes: Rounding Whole Numbers

Questions to Consider About the Key Mathematical Concepts

Do students understand how to round whole numbers to a given place value? To what extent, do they

- correctly apply ideas of place value including identifying the digit in a particular place in a numeral?
- apply a rounding strategy such as reasoning about a digit's value or applying rounding rules?

Common Core Connection (3.NBT)

Grade: Third

Domain: Number and Operations—Base Ten

Cluster:

A. Use place value understanding and properties of operations to perform multi-digit arithmetic.

3.NBT.A.1. Use place value understanding to round whole numbers to the nearest 10 or 100.

Uncovering Student Understanding About the Key Concepts

Using the Rounding Whole Numbers Probe can provide the following information about how students are thinking about place value and rounding to the nearest 10 or 100.

Do they		*Do they*
- read whole numbers in a way that shows understanding of place value; for example, 439 as "four hundred thirty nine"?	OR	- read whole numbers without place value or with incorrect place value such as reading 439 as "forty-three nine"?
- understand the structure and names of the whole number place values?	OR	- get confused about the value of a digit in a certain place value?

- know the relationship between adjacent places in a numeral—that a digit one place to the left is worth 10 times as much as the digit?

OR

- lack understanding of the relationship of digits in different place value locations?

- reason about the value of a number compared to its value rounded to another place value and apply rounding convention?

OR

- misapply rounding rules?

Exploring Excerpts From Educational Resources and Related Research

Common areas of difficulty for students:

Rounding to the unit represented by the leftmost place is typically the sort of estimate that is easiest for students. Rounding to the unit represented by a place in the middle of a number may be more difficult for students (the surrounding digits are sometimes distracting). (Common Core Standards Writing Team, 2012a, p. 11)

Data from the Mathematics Assessment for Learning and Teaching (MaLT) project data base indicate that students have difficulty with rounding. These difficulties include rounding some but not all numbers and viewing rounding as truncating such as rounding 68 to 60. (Ryan & Williams, 2007, p. 191)

Surveying the Prompts and Selected Responses in the Probe

The Probe consists of six selected response prompts, each with four possible choices, and an explanation. The prompts and selected responses are designed to elicit understandings and common difficulties as described below.

If a student chooses	It is likely that the student
1. b 2. a 3. d 4. c 5. a 6. d (correct responses)	• can identify the digit in the named place value and reason about the digit to its right in order to round the whole number and can apply rounding conventions [See Sample Student Responses 1 and 2]. *Look for indication of the student's understanding in the written explanations of how the student got the answer.*

(Continued)

(Continued)

If a student chooses	It is likely that the student
1. a 2. b 3. c 5. a 6. a	• is viewing rounding as truncating, always rounding down or does not apply common rounding convention for the digit 5.
2. b or c 3. b or d 4. a or b 5. d 6. b or c	• is rounding correctly or incorrectly to a different place.
1. c or d 4. d 5. b	• can identify the digit in the named place value and reason about the digit to its right in order to round the digit in the named place but only changes the number directly to the right to a 0; or • only changes the number in the given place and keeps the numbers following as is [See Sample Student Response 4].

Teaching Implications and Considerations

Ideas for eliciting more information from students about their understanding and difficulties:

- If students have selected the correct answers, ask clarifying questions as needed about their explanations. Look for evidence of understanding of place value and evidence of whether the student is merely applying rounding rules or if there is conceptual understanding of these rules. Consider questions such as, How do you decide whether to round up or down? What numbers is this number between?
- For students with errors, ask questions to learn about their approach:
  - How did you decide how to round this number?
  - Is this number more or less than ____? How do you know?
  - Was one of these rounding problems easier for you? More difficult?

Ideas for planning instruction in response to what you learned from the results of administering the Probe:

- Provide practice and visuals to help students distinguish between the similarities and differences of place value names.
- Use concrete manipulatives such as base-ten blocks or bundles to build meaning of the digit to the left as 10 times greater.
- Use number lines to consider the proximity of numbers to other numbers and build the idea that rounding to the nearest means selecting the number that is closer on the number line.

- Build student understanding of the goal of rounding to the nearest: "to approximate the number by the closest number with no ones or no tens and ones (e.g., so 456 to the nearest ten is 460; and to the nearest hundred is 500)" (Common Core Standards Writing Team, 2011a, p. 11).

Sample Student Responses to Rounding Whole Numbers

Responses That Suggest Understanding

Sample Student Response 1

Student chose "a. 400" for Problem 2 and wrote, "439 is closer to 400 than it is to 500."

Sample Student Response 2

Student chose "d. 9,840" for Problem 6 and wrote, "There's a 3 in the tens place. This is the place I have to round to. The ones place will be a 0 when I round. So the answer has to be 9,830 or 9,840. The rule is to round up when there is a 5, so I picked 9,840."

Responses That Suggest Difficulty

Sample Student Response 3

Student chose "d. 299" for Problem 1 and wrote, "Since there is a 9 in the tens place that is going to round up in the hundreds place so it's 299."

Sample Student Response 4

Student chose "b. 2,300" for Problem 3 and wrote, "Since there is a 4 after the 3, I rounded off."

Subtracting Whole Numbers

Determine if the answer to the subtraction problem is correct.

Circle Correct or NOT Correct:	Show or tell why:
A. $\begin{array}{r} 4\ \ 3\ \ 8 \\ -\ 2\ \ 4\ \ 6 \\ \hline 2\ \ 1\ \ 2 \end{array}$ Correct NOT Correct	
B. $\begin{array}{r} 7\ \ 0\ \ 4 \\ -\ 3\ \ 5\ \ 6 \\ \hline 3\ \ 4\ \ 8 \end{array}$ Correct NOT Correct	
C. $\begin{array}{r} 5\ \ 1\ \ 3 \\ -\ 3\ \ 2\ \ 7 \\ \hline 1\ \ 9\ \ 6 \end{array}$ Correct NOT Correct	

Teacher Notes: Subtracting Whole Numbers

Questions to Consider About the Key Mathematical Concepts

Do students understand subtraction based on place value and/or reasoning about the relationship between addition and subtraction? To what extent, do they

- apply strategies for subtracting whole numbers based on place value, including regrouping as necessary?
- judge the reasonableness of their answers demonstrating place value understanding and understanding of the operation?

Common Core Connection (3.NBT)

Grade: Third

Domain: Number and Operations—Base Ten

Cluster:

A. Use place value understanding and properties of operations to perform multi-digit arithmetic.

3.NBT.A.2. Fluently add and subtract within 1,000 using strategies and algorithms based on place value, properties of operations, and/or the relationship between addition and subtraction.

Uncovering Student Understanding About the Key Concepts

Using the Subtracting Whole Numbers Probe can provide the following information about how students are thinking about the effect of the operation on the numbers involved.

Do they

- apply understanding of key number and operations ideas to facilitate subtraction, such as
  - o demonstrating place value understanding of a three-digit number?

OR

Do they

- treat each place value pair as a separate subtraction problem?
- subtract the smaller digit from the larger digit without regard to position?

- commutativity and associativity?
- composition and decomposition (regrouping)?

Do they

- make mistakes with regrouping, not conserving the value of the number?

Exploring Excerpts From Educational Resources and Related Research

Common areas of difficulty for students:

A number of error patterns exist when students subtract whole numbers including: treating each position as a separate subtraction problem; thinking of the larger number as the set and the smaller as the subset regardless of position; and errors with regrouping. (Ashlock, 2006, pp. 113 and 118)

Research studies, national reports, and international comparisons have for decades identified many aspects of computation in which children's performances was [*sic*] disappointing. For example, on standardized tests the U.S. Grade 2 norm for two-digit subtraction requiring regrouping (e.g., 62 − 48) is 38% correct. Many children subtract the smaller from the larger in each column to get 26 as the answer to 62 − 48. This top-from-bottom error is largely eliminated when children learn to subtract with understanding. (NCTM, 2003, p. 71)

Children make many different errors in adding and subtracting multidigit numbers, and many students who add or subtract correctly cannot explain how they got their answers. (NCTM, 2003, p. 79)

Surveying the Prompts and Selected Responses in the Probe

The Probe consists of three items, each with two choices. The prompts and selected responses are designed to elicit understandings and common difficulties as described below.

If a student chooses	*It is likely that the student*
A. Not correct B. Correct C. Not correct	• is applying correct subtraction strategies [See Sample Student Responses 1 and 2]. *Look for indication of the student's understanding in the written explanations of how the student got the answer.*

If a student chooses	It is likely that the student

A. Correct
B. Not correct
C. Correct
	• has one or more of the following errors:
	   ○ subtracting smaller number from larger regardless of order [See Sample Student Response 3].
	   ○ incorrect decomposition and recomposition approaches such as not reducing a digit by one 10 or one 100 when regrouping.
	   ○ has difficulties with regrouping when there are no 10s [See Sample Student Response 4].

Teaching Implications and Considerations

Ideas for eliciting more information from students about their understanding and difficulties:

- What is the value of this digit? [Point to a particular digit to determine whether students include the place value; e.g., point to the "5" in 356 and listen for "5 tens" or "50" rather than "5."]
- For students who disregard order, ask questions that use smaller numbers such as, "If you were to subtract 8 from 15, would you get 3?"
- How can you check the reasonableness of your results?

Ideas for planning instruction in response to what you learned from the results of administering the Probe:

- Use base-ten blocks or other concrete bundles of 100, 10, and 1 to build understanding of renaming numbers. Provide multiple opportunities to subtract numbers involving zeros using these concrete models.
- When building understanding of the algorithm, focus on subtraction as takeaway rather than comparison.
- Build students' ability to determine whether regrouping is necessary.
- Provide many experiences with estimating results of subtracting so students are able to judge the reasonableness of their calculations.
- "The main focus in teaching the standard algorithm is not as a memorized process but as making sense of the procedure as a process." (Van de Walle et al., 2013, p. 219)

Sample Student Responses to Subtracting Whole Numbers

Responses That Suggest Understanding

Sample Student Response 1

Student chose "Not correct" on Problem A and wrote, "The number in the tens place of the answer is not a 1. In order to do this part of the subtraction, you have to regroup 10 tens. The answer is 192."

(Continued)

(Continued)

Sample Student Response 2

Student chose "Correct" on Problem C and wrote, "I checked by adding and 196 + 327 = 523 not 513."

Responses That Suggest Difficulty

Sample Student Response 3

Student chose "Correct" on Problem A and wrote, "This is right because when you subtract each place it comes out. 4 − 2 = 2 4 − 3 −1 and 8 − 6 = 2."

Sample Student Response 4

Student chose "Not correct" on Problem B and wrote:

$$\begin{array}{r} {}^{6}\!\!\not{7}04 \\ -\ 356 \\ \hline 358 \end{array}$$

Are They Equivalent?

Without actually calculating, use what you know about multiplying two-digit numbers to decide which of the number expressions below are equivalent to

24 × 16

	Circle one:	Explain your answer:
A. **16 × 24**	Yes No	
B. **26 × 14**	Yes No	
C. **(20 + 4) × 16**	Yes No	
D. **12 × 32**	Yes No	
E. **42 × 61**	Yes No	

Teacher Notes: Are They Equivalent?

Questions to Consider About the Key Mathematical Concepts

Do students understand how ideas of whole number decomposition and commutativity can be used to evaluate whether or not multiplication expressions are equivalent? To what extent, do they

- apply ideas of whole number decomposition and commutativity to rewrite an expression?
- apply an understanding of place value and the operation of multiplication to determine whether number expressions are equivalent?

Common Core Connection (4.NBT)

Grade: Fourth

Domain: Number and Operations—Base Ten

Cluster:

B. Use place value understanding and properties of operations to perform multi-digit arithmetic.

4.NBT.B.5. Multiply a whole number of up to four digits by a 1-digit whole number, and multiply two 2-digit numbers, using strategies based on place value and the properties of operations. Illustrate and explain the calculation by using equations, rectangular arrays, and/or area models.

Uncovering Student Understanding About the Key Concepts

Using the Are They Equivalent? Probe can provide the following information about how students are thinking about place value considerations for multiplication of two-digit numerals.

Do they

- understand that changing the position of digits *within* a two- or three-digit numeral will change the value of that numeral, except in cases where that digit is the same?

OR

Do they

- change positions of digits without regard to the value of the digit determined by its position within the numeral?

Do they

- apply understanding of multiplication and reasoning such as composition and decomposition, commutativity, associativity, and estimation to determine equivalence?

OR

Do they

- rely on computation using an algorithm rather than reasoning about the size of the numbers and the effect of the operation of multiplication?

Exploring Excerpts From Educational Resources and Related Research

Common areas of difficulty for students:

Students and teachers have found learning and teaching place value difficult. This difficulty is related to the complexity of our numeration system. Understanding place value requires understanding a variety of mathematical properties including the additive, positional, base-ten and multiplicative properties. (Ross, 2002, p. 419)

Place value is one basis for flexible decomposition and recomposition of number, a key element in other skills related to number sense—mental computation and estimation. (Battista, 2002, p. 83)

Flexible methods for computation require a strong understanding of the operations and properties of the operations, especially the commutative property and the associative property. . . . Flexible methods for computing, especially mental methods, allow students to reason much more effectively in every area of mathematics involving numbers. (Van de Walle et al., 2013, p. 216)

Surveying the Prompts and Selected Responses in the Probe

The justified list Probe consists of one prompt followed by five yes-or-no items designed to assess understanding of equivalent expressions, properties of multiplication, and place value. The prompts and selected responses are designed to elicit understandings and common difficulties as described below.

If a student chooses	It is likely that the student
A, C, D (equivalent expressions)	- is able to apply ideas of decomposition, commutativity, and associativity to reason about equivalent expressions [See Sample Student Response 1]. *Look for indication of the student's understanding in the written explanations of how the student got the answer.*

(Continued)

(Continued)

If a student chooses	It is likely that the student
B and/or E (Yes)	• applies a concept that is true for the operation of addition without consideration to the impact of multiplication [See Sample Student Response 2]. • does not consider that the location of a digit within a numeral determines its value.
C and/or D (No)	• does not apply understanding of decomposing 24 and/or distribution [See Sample Student Response 3]. • does not apply understanding of factors and equivalent expressions and/or associativity.

Teaching Implications and Considerations

Ideas for eliciting more information from students about their understanding and difficulties:

- For students who have answered the prompts correctly but whose explanations are not clear or complete, ask them to explain how they determined whether expressions were or were not equivalent. Listen for understanding of place value and reasoning about the operation of multiplication.
- To learn more about students' thinking, ask questions such as

  ○ "How did you decide on your responses?"
  ○ "What does it mean for two expressions to be equivalent?"
  ○ "Can you think of another expression that is equivalent to this one?"

Ideas for planning instruction in response to what you learned from the results of administering the Probe:

- Use visual area models and strategies such as the box method that help to reinforce ideas of decomposition and place value.
- Help students build the meaning of equivalence as an alternative way of expressing the same quantity. Connect equivalent expressions to other examples of equivalence, such as equivalent fractions or whole number decomposition sentences.
- Provide experiences with physical models: introducing groupable (individual units such as straws that can be bundled together) models first and proportionally pre-grouped (such as base-ten blocks) models play a key role in helping students understand 10 ones as "ten" as well as 10 tens as "hundred." (Van de Walle et al., 2013, p. 195)
- Students need experiences in noting how using concrete representations of a number differ from numeric representations. Especially important is understanding that the arrangements of the digits in the numeric representation matters (the digit in the 10's is to the left of the digit in the 1's) whereas when concrete models are used the value is not determined by the arrangement of the materials. (NCTM, 2000, p. 81)

Sample Student Responses to Are They Equivalent?

Responses That Suggest Understanding

Sample Student Response 1

Student circled "Yes" for Problem C and wrote, "24 is the same as 20 + 4 and if you add these first before multiplying you get 24 × 16."

Responses That Suggest Difficulty

Sample Student Response 2

Student circled "Yes" for Problem B and wrote, "6 × 4 and 4 × 6 are the same and 2 × 1 and 1 × 2 are the same."

Sample Student Response 3

Student circled "No" for Problem D and wrote, "This is not the same numbers so it can't be equal."

Variation: Are They Equivalent?

1. Without adding the two numbers, use what you know about adding 3-digit numbers to decide which of the number expressions below are equivalent to

427 + 569

	Circle one:	Explain your answer:
A. **724 + 965**	Yes No	
B. **467 + 529**	Yes No	
C. **527 + 469**	Yes No	
D. **472 + 596**	Yes No	
E. **927 + 69**	Yes No	

2. Without subtracting the two numbers, use what you know about subtracting 3-digit numbers to decide which of the number expressions below are equivalent to

618 – 498

	Circle one:	Explain your answer:
A. **620 – 500**	Yes No	
B. **681 – 489**	Yes No	
C. **608 – 488**	Yes No	
D. **698 – 418**	Yes No	
E. **618 – 418 – 80**	Yes No	

Rounding Decimals

3.4

1. **Circle the letter that shows the value of 18.75 rounded to the nearest *whole number*:**

a. 20　　　　b. 18.8　　　　c. 19.75　　　　d. 19　　　　e. 18

Explain your choice:

2. **Circle the letter that shows the value of 55.729 rounded to the nearest *tenth*:**

a. 55.7　　　　b. 65.729　　　　c. 55.73　　　　d. 55.8　　　　e. 60

Explain your choice:

3. **Circle the letter that shows the value of 99.827 rounded to the nearest *hundredth*:**

a. 99.825　　　　b. 100　　　　c. 99.83　　　　d. 99.82　　　　e. 100.83

Explain your choice:

Teacher Notes: Rounding Decimals

Questions to Consider About the Key Mathematical Concepts

Do students understand rounding decimals as a way of estimating numbers in which you increase or decrease the value of the number to a given place? To what extent do they

- correctly apply ideas of place value including identifying the digit in a particular place in a numeral?
- apply a rounding strategy such as reasoning about a digit's value or applying rounding rules?

Common Core Connection (5.NBT)

Grade: Fifth

Domain: Number and Operations–Base Ten

Cluster:

A. Understand the place value system.

5.NBT.A.4. Use place value understanding to round decimals to any place.

Uncovering Student Understanding About the Key Concepts

Using the Rounding Decimals Probe can provide the following information about how students are thinking about decimal place value:

Do they		*Do they*
- understand that decimal fractions are an extension of whole numbers?	OR	- view decimals as completely different from whole numbers?
- read decimals as fractions in a way that shows understanding of place value; for example, 2.3 as "two and three tenths"?	OR	- only read a decimal one way (e.g., 2.3 as "two point three")?

Do they

- understand the structure of decimals and the names of the place values to the left and to the right of the decimal point?

OR

- understand the relationship between adjacent places in a numeral—that a digit one place to the right is worth one tenth of its value in the current place *and* that a digit moved one place to the left is worth ten times its value?

OR

- reason about the value of a number compared to its value rounded to another place value?

OR

Do they

- get confused about the value of a digit in a certain place value location?

- lack understanding of the relationship of digits in different place value locations?

- misapply rounding rules?

Exploring Excerpts From Educational Resources and Related Research

Common areas of difficulty for students:

Most students do not develop sufficient meanings for decimal symbols when they are introduced. Soon students are asked to learn rules for manipulating decimals. Because they do not know what the symbols mean, they have no way of figuring out why the rules work. (Hiebert, 2002, p. 119)

The decimal point is used to signify the location of the ones place, but its location may suggest there should be a "oneths" place to its right in order to create symmetry with respect to the decimal point. However, because one is the basic unit from which the other base-ten units are derived, the symmetry occurs instead with the ones place. (Common Core Standards Writing Team, 2012a, p. 12)

The naming of decimal numbers needs special attention. The place-value name for 0.642 is six hundred forty-two *thousandths*. Compare this form with 642, where we simply say six hundred forty-two, not 642 ones. This source of confusion is compounded by the use of the *dths* (thousand*ths*, hundred*ths*) or *nths* (ten*ths*) with decimal numbers and the use of *d* (thousan*d*, hundre*d*) or *n* (te*n*) with whole numbers [italics in original]. The additional digits in the whole number with a similar name is another source of confusion. Whereas 0.642 is read 642 thousand*ths*, 642,000 is read 642 thousan*d* meaning 642 thousand *ones*. (Sowder, 2002, p. 114)

Surveying the Prompts and Selected Responses in the Probe

The Probe consists of three selected response prompts, each with five possible choices, and an explanation. The prompts and selected responses are designed to elicit understandings and common difficulties as described below.

If a student chooses	It is likely that the student
1. d 2. a 3. c (correct answers)	• can identify the digit in the named place value and reason about the digit to its right in order to round the decimal fraction [See Sample Student Response 1]. *Look for indication of the student's understanding in the written explanations of how the student got the answer.*
1. a, b, or c 2. c 3. a	• confuses place values or what it means to round and rounds to the wrong place [See Sample Student Response 2].
2. b or e 3. b or e	• confuses ten*ths* and ten*s* and/or hundred*ths* and hundred*s* [See Sample Student Response 3].
1. e 2. d 3. d	• confuses rounding rules or reasons incorrectly about the size of the decimal and has rounded up instead of down, or down instead of up [See Sample Student Response 4].

Teaching Implications and Considerations

Ideas for eliciting more information from students about their understanding and difficulties:

• If students have selected the correct answers, ask clarifying questions as needed about their explanations. Look for evidence of understanding of place value and evidence of whether the student is merely applying rounding rules or whether there is conceptual understanding of these rules. Consider questions such as, How do you decide whether to round up or down? Can you tell me two numbers that this number is between?

- For students with errors, ask questions to learn about their approach:
  - How did you decide how to round this number?
  - Is this number more or less than—? How do you know?
  - Was one of these rounding problems easier for you? More difficult?

Ideas for planning instruction in response to what you learned from the results of administering the Probe:

- Spend time building the meaning of decimals and what it means to round a number to a given place. Concrete materials such as base-ten blocks and hundredths grid paper or hundredths disks can help students gain a sense of the relative size of decimals and the relationship between place values.
- Ask students to draw decimals on grid paper or to plot decimals on a number line to provide visual explanation for rounding up and down rules.
- Help students understand that decimal fractions are an extension of our whole number system and use place value charts as a visual tool and reminder.
- Provide practice and visuals to help students distinguish between the similarities and differences of place value names.

Sample Student Responses to Rounding Decimals

Responses That Suggest Difficulty

Sample Student Response 1

Student chose "d. 19" for Problem 1 and wrote, "I chose 19 because $18\frac{3}{4}$ is closer to 19 than it is to 10 or 18. The other choices were not whole numbers so they can't be right."

Responses That Suggest Understanding

Sample Student Response 2

Student chose "c. 19.75" on Problem 1, and wrote

.730 = .73.

.729 is one thousandth from .73.

Sample Student Response 3

Student chose "e. 60" on Problem 2 and wrote, "I think 60 because it's part of the 10's."

Sample Student Response 4

Student chose "b. 65.729" on Problem 2 and wrote, "I think that b is the answer because it is closer to 55.729."

Adding Decimals

Three students added **0.14 + 2.9**

Their work is shown below:

```
  0 . 1 4            0 . 1  4           0 . 1 4
+ 2 . 9            +     2 . 9        + 2 . 9
---------          -----------        ---------
  2 . 1 0 4            4 . 3             3 . 0 4
```

Taylor

Shawn

Jeremy

	Do you agree or disagree with the work?	Explain why:
Taylor	Agree Disagree	
Shawn	Agree Disagree	
Jeremy	Agree Disagree	

Teacher Notes: Adding Decimals

Questions to Consider About the Key Mathematical Concepts

Do students apply an understanding of place value when adding decimals? To what extent, do they

- combine digits based on their place value?
- consider the reasonableness of a solution when evaluating its accuracy?
- write explanations that reflect an understanding of addition and place value?

Common Core Connection (5.NBT)

Grade: 5

Domain: Number and Operations–Base Ten

Cluster:

B. Perform operations with multi-digit whole numbers and with decimals to hundredths.

5.NBT.B.7. Add, subtract, multiply, and divide decimals to hundredths, using concrete models or drawings and strategies based on place value, properties of operations, and/or the relationship between addition and subtraction; relate the strategy to a written method and explain the reasoning used.

Uncovering Student Understanding About the Key Concepts

Using the Adding Decimals Probe can provide the following information about how students are thinking about decimal addition.

Do they

- understand the relationship between adjacent place values and that only like parts can be combined?

OR

- use estimation or rounding to determine whether answers are reasonable?

Do they

- disregard place value when evaluating a sum?

OR

- apply a procedure without reasoning about the size of the addends and the sum?

Do they		*Do they*
• interpret the meaning of the decimal point and understand that the location of digit within a decimal determines its value?	OR	• treat decimals as though they are whole numbers?

Exploring Excerpts From Educational Resources and Related Research

Common areas of difficulty for students:

Data from the Mathematics Assessment for Learning and Teaching (MaLT) project data base indicate that students have difficulty with decimal addition. These difficulties include treating the decimal part as though it is a separate whole number. For example, they would add 0.65 + 0.2 and get a sum of 0.67. The data showed that 13% of fourteen-year-olds held this misconception. (Ryan & Williams, 2007, p. 217)

Most students do not develop sufficient meanings for decimal symbols when they are introduced. Soon students are asked to learn rules for manipulating decimals. Because they do not know what the symbols mean, they have no way of figuring out why the rules work. They must memorize each rule and hope that they remember on which problems to use them, a method that works for the simplest routine problems that are practiced heavily but not for problems that are even a little different. Without knowing what the symbols mean, students are unable to judge whether their answers are reasonable or whether they are on the right track. (Hiebert, 2002, p. 119)

Surveying the Prompts and Selected Responses in the Probe

This Probe consists of three examples of student work on a decimal addition problem, along with an agree/disagree choice and explanation for each student work sample. The sample student responses reflect common difficulties as described below.

If a student chooses	*It is likely that the student*
Taylor: Disagree Shawn: Disagree Jeremy: Agree (correct answers)	• understands how to perform decimal addition, in particular the importance of adding tenths to tenths and hundredths to hundredths and of regrouping [See Sample Student Response 1].

(Continued)

(Continued)

If a student chooses	It is likely that the student
	• uses reasoning about the size of the addends to choose the correct sum. *Look for indication of the student's understanding in the written explanations of how the student got the answer.*
Taylor—Agree	• disregards place value and regrouping when adding .1 and .9 [See Sample Student Response 5].
Shawn—Disagree	• treats decimals as though they are whole numbers with the decimal point separating the two sides or combines digits without paying attention to regrouping [See Sample Student Response 4].

*T*eaching Implications and Considerations

Ideas for eliciting more information from students about their understanding and difficulties:

- How did you decide whether you agreed or disagreed with a student's thinking?
- What do you think about when you are adding decimals? In what ways is adding decimals like adding whole numbers?

Ideas for planning instruction in response to what you learned from the results of administering the Probe:

- Use concrete materials such as base-ten blocks and hundredths grid paper to model decimals and decimal addition and to build understanding of place value and regrouping.
- Ask students to estimate sums and incorporate estimation into computation routines. Estimation helps students to check the reasonableness of their answer and to build understanding of the algorithm.
- Use language that helps build place value understanding. Calling 0.14 "fourteen hundredths" rather than "point one four" and 0.2 "two-tenths" rather than "point 2" may help students avoid the common error of thinking that "point one four" plus "point two" is "point sixteen."

Sample Student Responses to Adding Decimals

Responses That Suggest Understanding

Sample Student Response 1

Student agreed with Jeremy and wrote, "He's adding the right places. .1 + .9 = 1.0, then add the .04 of the .14.

  2.0 + 1.0 + .04 = 3.04

Sample Student Response 2

Student disagreed with Taylor and wrote, ".104 is less than 0.14, so it doesn't make sense that you would get .104 as a sum of 0.14 and .9: 0.14 +.9 = 1.04."

Responses That Suggest Difficulty

Sample Student Response 3

Student disagreed with Taylor and wrote, "14 + 9 = 23 not 104."

Sample Student Response 4

Student disagreed with Shawn and wrote, "1 + 2 = 3 not 4. The answer should say 3.3, not 4.3."

Sample Student Response 5

Student agreed with Taylor and wrote,

  0 + 2 = 2,

  10 + 90 = 100 + 4 = 104.

Variation: Subtracting Decimals

Three students subtracted **5.83 − 1.9**

Their work is shown below.

```
  5 . 8 3          5 . 8 3          5 . 8 3
- 1 . 9          - 1 . 9 0        -     1 9
─────────        ─────────        ─────────
  4 . 1 3          3 . 9 3          5 . 6 4
```

Adelyn   Kim   Betsy

	Do you agree or disagree with the work?	Explain why:
Adelyn	Agree Disagree	
Kim	Agree Disagree	
Betsy	Agree Disagree	

Decimal Division Estimates

<u>Without calculating</u>, use mental math and/or estimation to determine the estimate for each division problem.

Circle one:	Explain your choice:
1. **5.4 ÷ 0.6** The quotient is a. between 0.5 and 1 b. between 5 and 10 c. between 50 and 100	
2. **19.6 ÷ 0.05** The quotient is a. between 3 and 4 b. between 30 and 40 c. between 300 and 400	

Teacher Notes: Decimal Division Estimates

Questions to Consider About the Key Mathematical Concepts

When solving problems involving the division of decimal fractions, can students reason about the size of the numbers and the effect of the operation in order to determine a reasonable estimate? To what extent, do they

- reason correctly about the size of the divisor and dividend?
- determine whether the quotient will be smaller or larger than the dividend?
- describe how to use this reasoning to determine a reasonable estimate?

Common Core Connection (5.NBT)

Grade: 5

Domain: Numbers and Operations in Base Ten

Cluster:

B. Perform operations with multi-digit whole numbers and with decimals to hundredths.

5.NBT.B.7. Add, subtract, multiply, and divide decimals to hundredths, using concrete models or drawings and strategies based on place value, properties of operations, and/or the relationship between addition and subtraction; relate the strategy to a written method and explain the reasoning used.

Uncovering Student Understanding About the Key Concepts

Using the Decimal Division Estimates Probe can provide the following information about how students are thinking about the effect of dividing with decimals.

Do they
- correctly reason about the size of the dividend and divisor?

OR

Do they
- apply incorrect place value thinking?

- correctly reason about the size of the quotient?

OR

- apply an overgeneralization of "division always results in a smaller answer"?

- use reasoning about the size of the decimals and the effect of the division?

OR

- revert to applying an algorithm rather than using reasoning to determine an estimate?

*E*xploring Excerpts From Educational Resources and Related Research

Common areas of difficulty for students:

Multiplying and dividing fractions and decimals can be challenging for many students because of problems that are primarily conceptual rather than procedural. From their experience with whole numbers, many students appear to develop a belief that "multiplication makes bigger and division makes smaller." (NCTM, 2000, p. 218)

Errors show that many students have learned rules for manipulating symbols without understanding what those symbols mean or why the rules work. Many students are unable to reason appropriately about symbols for rational numbers and do not have the strategic competence that would allow them to catch their mistakes. (NRC, 2001, p. 234)

Developing fluency requires a balance and connection between conceptual understanding and computational proficiency. Computational methods that are over-practiced without understanding are often forgotten or remembered incorrectly. (Hiebert 1999; Kamii, Lewis, and Livingston 1993; Hiebert and Lindquist 1990). (NCTM, 2000, p. 35)

*S*urveying the Prompts and Selected Responses in the Probe

The Probe consists of two selected response items, each with three choices. The prompts and selected responses are designed to elicit understandings and common difficulties as described below.

If a student chooses	It is likely that the student
1. b 2. c (correct responses)	• reasons about the size of the decimals and the effect of the operation; or • applies an algorithm rather than using reasoning to determine an estimate [See Sample Student Response 1]. *Look for indication of the student's understanding in the written explanations of how the student got the answer.*
1. a 2. b	• is applying the incorrect assumption that "division always makes smaller." [See Sample Student Response 2].
1. c 2. a	• incorrectly applies an algorithm rather than using reasoning to determine an estimate; or • shows partial or inconsistent reasoning about either the size of the decimal or the effect of the operation [See Sample Student Response 3].

Teaching Implications and Considerations

Ideas for eliciting more information from students about their understanding and difficulties:

- For students who incorrectly reason about the size of the decimals, ask, "What benchmark or whole number is this number close to?"
- For students who apply the "division makes smaller" rule, ask, "How can you model 2 divided by 0.5?" If they are able to correctly show that there are four "halves" in 2, follow up with, "How can this help you think about these problems?"
- For students who apply an algorithm rather than estimating, ask, "How might you think about this without actually calculating an answer?"

Ideas for planning instruction in response to what you learned from the results of administering the Probe:

- Use representations and concrete models such as number lines and base-ten blocks to help students understand division as "How many — are in —?" or "— has how many —?"
- Use hundredths grid shading, equivalent fraction benchmarks, and other strategies to help students build visual images of the magnitude of decimal numbers. (e.g., 0.53 is close to $\frac{1}{2}$, so I can think of 9.6 ÷ 0.53 as "how many one-halves are there in 10?")
- Provide a problem context to help students make sense of the division expression and reason about the results.

Sample Student Responses to Decimal Division Estimates

Responses That Suggest Understanding

Sample Student Response 1

Student chose "b" for Problem 1 and wrote, "Because if you round 5.4 down to 5 and 0.6 to 1.0, there are 5 ones in 5."

Responses That Suggest Difficulty

Sample Student Response 2

Student chose "a" for Problem 1 and wrote, "Why I think 'a' is because 5.4 is already close to 5 and then you are dividing, so it has to get smaller than 5."

Sample Student Response 3

Student chose "a" for Problem 1 and wrote, "I changed 5.4 ÷ .6 to a similar problem 54 ÷ 6 = 9. Then I put the decimal point back in to make the answer 0.9 which is between 0.5 and 1."

Variation: Division Estimates

<u>Without calculating</u>, use mental math and/or estimation to determine the best range of estimates of the quotient for each problem.

Circle ONE number from the Bigger Than list and ONE number from the Smaller Than list.	Explain your choices:
1. **25768 ÷ 49** Circle one: Bigger Than Circle one: Smaller Than 100 250 250 500 500 750	
2. **5934 ÷ 281** Circle one: Bigger Than Circle one: Smaller Than 10 100 100 200 200 500	

4

Number and Operations: Fractions Probes

The content of the Probes in this chapter aligns with the standards for Grades 3 through 5. The Probes and their variations will also be relevant beyond the aligned grade level for students in higher grades who have not yet met standards from previous grade levels, as well as for students who have already met the standards at their own grade level.

We developed these Probes to address the following critical areas of focus, described in the standards (CCSSO, 2010):

The content of the Probes in this chapter aligns with the standards for Grades 3 through 5. The Probes and their variations will also be relevant beyond the aligned grade level for students in higher grades who have not yet met standards from previous grade levels, as well as for students who have already met the standards at their own grade level.

- Develop understanding of fractions as numbers.
- Extend understanding of fraction equivalence.
- Understand decimal notation for fractions, and compare decimal fractions.
- Use equivalent fractions as a strategy to add and subtract fractions.

Remember to take a look at the variations that are available with some of the Probes in this chapter. All of these variations address number and operations ideas with fractions but may extend the idea or offer a different structure for administering them. When available, variation Probes follow the Teacher Notes and associated reproducibles for the related original Probe.

Common Core Math Content

Common Core Mathematical Content	Related Question	Probe Name
Understand a fraction as a number on the number line; represent fractions on a number line diagram. 3.NF.A.2	Do students understand a fraction as a number that can be represented on a number line?	Locating a Fraction on a Number Line (p. 98)
Explain equivalence of fractions in special cases, and compare fractions by reasoning about their size. 3.NF.A.3 Understand a fraction $\frac{1}{b}$ as the quantity formed by 1 part when a whole is partitioned into b equal parts; understand a fraction $\frac{a}{b}$ as the quantity formed by a parts of size $\frac{1}{b}$. 3.NF.A.1	Do students understand what it means for two fractions to be equivalent?	Equivalent Fractions Card Sort (p. 102) Variation: Equivalent or Not Equivalent? (p. 109)
Use decimal notation for fractions with denominators 10 or 100. For example, rewrite 0.62 as $\frac{62}{100}$; describe a length as 0.62 meters; locate 0.62 on a number line diagram. 4.NF.C.6	Do students understand that a decimal fraction (often shortened to decimal) is another way of expressing a fraction, and can be represented in a variety of ways?	Representing Decimals (p. 110)
Compare two fractions with different numerators and different denominators, e.g., by creating common denominators or numerators, or by comparing to a benchmark fraction such as $\frac{1}{2}$. Recognize that comparisons are valid only when the two fractions refer to the same whole. 4.NF.A.2	Do students understand fractions as a number, and are they able to reason about the size of a fraction in comparison to $\frac{1}{2}$?	Comparing to $\frac{1}{2}$ (p. 116) Variation: Comparing to $\frac{1}{2}$ (p. 121)
Understand a fraction $\frac{a}{b}$ with a > 1 as a sum of fractions $\frac{1}{b}$. 4.NF.B.3 Understand addition and subtraction of fractions as joining and separating parts referring to the same whole. 4.NF.B.3a	When solving problems involving estimation of the addition of two fractions, can students reason about the size of the numbers and the effect of the operation?	Fraction Estimates: Addition (p. 122) Variation: Fraction Estimates: Subtraction (p. 127)

Locating a Fraction on a Number Line

Three students are working together on a problem. They have different opinions about what to name the point shown on the number line below.

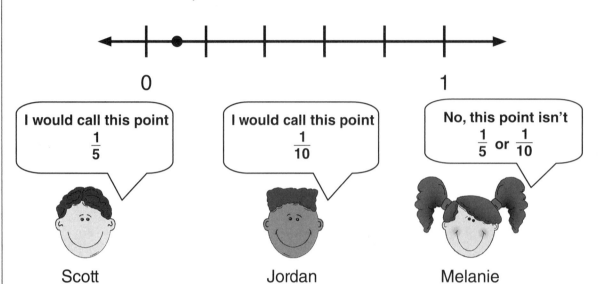

Who do you agree with?

Circle one: **Scott**   **Jordan**   **Melanie**

Explain your choice:

Teacher Notes: Locating a Fraction on a Number Line

Questions to Consider About the Key Mathematical Concepts

Do students understand a fraction as a number that can be represented on a number line? To what extent, do they

- reason about the size of the intervals given the whole?
- determine the location of the fraction?

Common Core Connection (3.NF)

Grade: Third

Domain: Number and Operations–Fractions

Cluster:

A. Develop understanding of fractions as numbers.

3.NF.A.2. Understand a fraction as a number on the number line; represent fractions on a number line diagram.

Uncovering Student Understanding About the Key Concepts

Using the Locating a Fraction on a Number Line Probe can provide the following information about how students are thinking about a fraction as a number that can be represented by a point on a number line.

Do they		*Do they*
• refer to the size of the intervals?	OR	• simply count the hash marks?
• further partition the fifths into tenths?	OR	• use nonequal-size intervals (considers the point as a hash mark, dividing the line into six intervals)?

Exploring Excerpts From Educational Resources and Related Research

Common areas of difficulty for students:

Children as late as 7th grade are unable to conceptualize a fraction as a point on a number line. Challenges include interpreting the unit on the number line and unit subdivisions that are not equal in number to the denominator (Larson, 1980). Number lines that are one unit in length tend to enable students to use the part whole model because they view the number line as a "whole" unit. (Martinie, 2007, p. 36)

Students sometimes have difficulty perceiving the unit on a number line diagram. When locating a fraction on a number line diagram, they might use as the unit the entire portion of the number line that is shown on the diagram, for example indicating the number 3 when asked to show $\frac{3}{4}$ on a number line diagram marked from 0 to 4. (Common Core Standards Writing Team, 2011b, p. 3 NF)

Surveying the Prompts and Selected Responses in the Probe

The Probe consists of one prompt and several choices in the "math-talk" format. The prompts and selected responses are designed to elicit understandings and common difficulties as described below.

If a student chooses	It is likely that the student
Jordan (correct answer)	• understands that fifths can be further partitioned into tenths. • names the point correctly [See Sample Student Response 1]. *Look for indication of the student's understanding in the written explanations of how the student got the answer.*
Scott	• determines the point as located in the first of five intervals [See Sample Student Response 2]. • views $\frac{1}{5}$ as being smaller than $\frac{1}{10}$ [See Sample Student Response 3].
Melanie	• determines the fraction incorrectly for a number of different reasons including but not limited to counting all of the hash marks, counting each of the spaces, or counting the point as if it is a hash mark [See Sample Student Response 4].

*T*eaching Implications and Considerations

Ideas for eliciting more information from students about their understanding and difficulties:

- Can you explain how you determined the name for the point?
- What do the hash marks [*point to the vertical lines to clarify terminology*] represent on this number line?
- What is the size of an interval on this line? In other words, how would you describe the distance from one hash mark to the one next to it?
- How do you use the size of the interval to name the point?

Ideas for planning instruction in response to what you learned from the results of administering the Probe:

- Using un-partitioned, blank number lines, provide opportunities for students to partition and label number lines into various size intervals.
- Have students work in both directions, naming points on number lines and plotting points on number lines.
- Give students experiences with number lines whose marked endpoints are not zero and one; for example, use number lines that extend from 1 to 2, from 0 to 2, or from 3 to 5.

Sample Student Responses to Locating a Fraction on a Number Line

Responses That Suggest Understanding

Sample Student Response 1

Student chose "Jordan," and wrote, "I think $\frac{1}{5}$ is at the 1st line. It is 5th because of the 5 spaces from 0 to the 1. So cutting 5th in half would make the point $\frac{1}{10}$."

Responses That Suggest Difficulty

Sample Student Response 2

Student chose "Scott," and wrote, "The dot is in the first spot and there are 5 spots in all."

Sample Student Response 3

Student chose "Scott," and wrote, "$\frac{1}{5}$ is closer to 0 than $\frac{1}{10}$."

Sample Student Response 4

Student chose "Melanie," and wrote, "I think it is $\frac{1}{6}$ because I counted."

Equivalent Fractions Card Sort

(Reproducible student cards follow Teacher Notes on p. 107.)

Equivalent	Not Equivalent
A.	B. $\dfrac{1}{4}$
C. $\dfrac{1}{3}$	D. $\dfrac{4}{16}$
E. $\dfrac{1}{4}$	F. $\dfrac{2}{4}$
G. $\dfrac{2}{5}$	H. $\dfrac{8}{12}$ $\dfrac{4}{6}$

I. $\dfrac{3}{8}$	J.
K. $\dfrac{2}{3}$ $\dfrac{4}{6}$	L.
M. $\dfrac{2}{5}$ $\dfrac{3}{5}$	N. $\dfrac{4}{8}$ $\dfrac{4}{6}$
O. $\dfrac{4}{8}$ $\dfrac{6}{8}$	P. $\dfrac{3}{6}$ $\dfrac{3}{8}$

Advance Preparation: Create cards by photocopying and cutting. Separate the label cards (Equivalent and NOT Equivalent) from the deck and shuffle the rest of the cards.

Instructions:

1. Invite the students to sort the cards into two piles: **Equivalent** and **NOT Equivalent**. Use the label cards to identify the piles.

2. As students finish the sort, give them the blank cards and ask them to create their own Equivalent and NOT Equivalent examples (have each student create one of each).

3. Either choose three cards for the students or ask the students to choose three cards from the Equivalent pile. Ask the students to explain how they knew these cards should go in the Equivalent pile.

4. Either choose three cards for the students or ask the students to choose three cards from the NOT Equivalent pile. Ask the students to explain how they knew these cards should go in the NOT Equivalent pile. Use the recording sheet as appropriate.

Teacher Notes: Equivalent Fractions Card Sort

Questions to Consider About the Key Mathematical Concepts

Do students understand what it means for two fractions to be equivalent? To what extent, do they

- demonstrate understanding of part-whole relationships through the use of area models?
- understand that, to be equivalent, the fractions must refer to the same-size whole?
- reason about the size of the parts when comparing two fractions?

Common Core Connection (3.NF)

Grade: Third

Domain: Number and Operations—Fractions

Cluster:

A. Develop understanding of fractions as numbers.

3.NF.A.1. Understand a fraction $\frac{1}{b}$ as the quantity formed by 1 part when a whole is partitioned into b equal parts; understand a fraction $\frac{a}{b}$ as the quantity formed by a parts of size $\frac{1}{b}$.

3.NF.A.3. Explain equivalence of fractions in special cases, and compare fractions by reasoning about their size.

Uncovering Student Understanding About the Key Concepts

Using the Equivalent Fractions Card Sort Probe can provide the following information about how students are thinking about area model and numeric representations of fractions.

Do they

- reason about the size of the fractions?   OR

- understand the represented parts must be of equal size?   OR

- refer to equivalent fractions as needing to refer to the same-size OR whole?

Do they

- compare either the numerators or the denominators as if they are separate whole numbers?

- count all shaded parts regardless of whether they are the same size?

- view equivalent fractions as having the same digit in the numerator and denominator?

Exploring Excerpts From Educational Resources and Related Research

Common areas of difficulty for students:

Using phrases such as "one out of two" or "one over three" when referring to part–whole relationships can contribute to student confusion. These phrases involve not only different language from that of partitioning but different images as well. (Siebert & Gaskin, 2006, p. 397)

Learning Pitfall: Applying whole number knowledge inappropriately to fractions. For example, students may look for one shaded out of two parts without understanding the need for congruent parts. (Bay Area Mathematics Task Force, 1999, p. 64)

Data from the Mathematics Assessment for Learning and Teaching (MaLT) project data base indicate that students have difficulty with recognizing fractions. These difficulties include viewing shapes divided into 4 unequal parts as $\frac{1}{4}$ and not recognizing equivalent fractions. (Ryan & Williams, 2007, pp. 192–193)

Surveying the Prompts and Selected Responses in the Probe

The Probe consists of sixteen cards with sets of examples and nonexamples to be sorted, and two blank cards. The prompts and selected responses are designed to elicit understandings and common difficulties as described below.

If a student chooses	*It is likely that the student*
A, D, E, F, G, H, K: Equivalent B, C, I, J, L, M, N, O, P: NOT Equivalent (correct answers)	• understands area model representations of fractions. • is able to reason about the size of the fractions in order to determine whether they are equivalent [See Sample Student Response 1]. *Look for indication of the student's understanding in the written explanations of how the student got the answer.*
Includes B, C, or I, as Equivalent	• does not understand that the size of the parts must be equal [See Sample Student Response 2].
Includes J as Equivalent	• compares parts needed to make a whole regardless of the different-size parts [See Sample Student Response 3].

If a student chooses	It is likely that the student
Includes M, N, O, or P as Equivalent OR Excludes H or K from Equivalent	• looks for either the digits in the numerators or in the denominators to be the same.
Excludes E or D from Equivalent	• is not familiar with varying the orientation or the position of the shaded parts.
Excludes G from Equivalent	• looks for only two parts shaded and five parts total, not yet understanding equivalent sets of parts to wholes [See Sample Student Response 4].

Teaching Implications and Considerations

Ideas for eliciting more information from students about their understanding and difficulties:

- What does it mean for two fractions to be *equivalent*?
- How did you determine whether the two fractions were equivalent?
- How could you represent each of these fractions with a visual model?
- What do the visual models tell you about how the size of the fractions compare?
- What is different about the shaded parts in these two models?

Ideas for planning instruction in response to what you learned from the results of administering the Probe:

- Use concrete area models such as circle pieces or fraction strips that allow students to see the part-to-whole relationship.
- When developing ideas related to part-to-whole relationships using area models, provide multiple experiences with varying the shapes used as the whole and with the orientation and position of the parts.
- Provide multiple experiences with various examples and nonexamples of given part-to-whole relationships.
- Help students understand that equivalent fractions are fractions that have the same overall value but they do not look exactly the same. Equivalent fractions represent the same part of the same-sized whole.
- Use interactive technology to connect visual and numeric representations.

Sample Student Responses to Equivalent Fractions Card Sort

Responses That Suggest Understanding

Sample Student Response 1

Student sorted all cards correctly. On one explanation, the student wrote, "Even though in 'J' both are $\frac{1}{4}$, the $\frac{1}{4}$ of the two shapes are different. The second shape is much bigger so $\frac{1}{4}$th in that shape is bigger than the $\frac{1}{4}$th in the first shape."

Responses That Suggest Difficulty

Sample Student Response 2

Student sorted Card "B" as Equivalent and wrote, "$\frac{1}{4}$ means 1 shaded out of 4 parts. That's what is shaded in the triangle."

Sample Student Response 3

Student sorted Card "J" as Equivalent and wrote, "Both have 1 more to make the whole circle complete."

Sample Student Response 4

Student sorted Card "G" as NOT Equivalent and wrote, "$\frac{2}{5}$ means is 2 shaded out of 5 total. The shape has 4 shaded out of 10 total which doesn't match."

Equivalent Fractions Cards

Equivalent	Not Equivalent
A.	B.
C. $\dfrac{1}{3}$	D. $\dfrac{4}{16}$
E. $\dfrac{1}{4}$	F. $\dfrac{2}{4}$
G. $\dfrac{2}{5}$	H. $\dfrac{8}{12}$ $\dfrac{4}{6}$

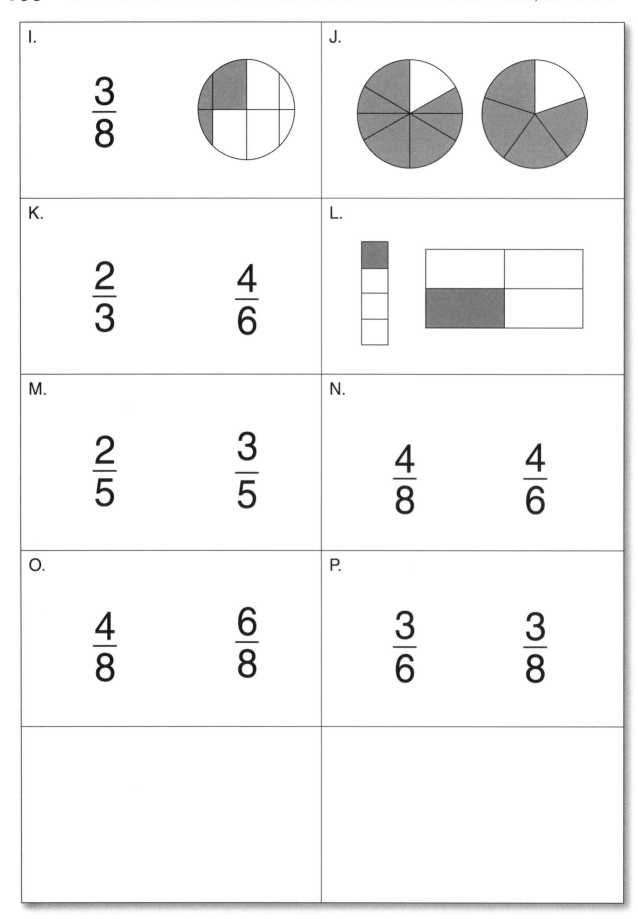

Variation: Equivalent or Not Equivalent?

Determine if the fractions are equivalent or not equivalent, and explain your choice.

	Circle one:	Explain your answer:
A. $\dfrac{2}{3}$ $\dfrac{4}{6}$	Equivalent NOT Equivalent	
B. $\dfrac{4}{6}$ $\dfrac{4}{8}$	Equivalent NOT Equivalent	
C. $\dfrac{5}{6}$ $\dfrac{7}{8}$	Equivalent NOT Equivalent	
D. $\dfrac{1}{3}$ $\dfrac{3}{9}$	Equivalent NOT Equivalent	

Representing Decimals

Which of the following are equivalent to **0.43**?

	Circle Yes or No:	Explain your answer:
A. **.04 + 0.3**	Yes No	
B. 0.4 ———•——— 0.5	Yes No	
C. (grid) $\square = \dfrac{1}{100}$	Yes No	

Which of the following are equivalent to **0.43**?

	Circle Yes or No:	Explain your answer:
D. $\dfrac{4}{10} + \dfrac{3}{100}$	Yes No	
E. $\dfrac{4}{3}$	Yes No	
F. **3 tenths and 13 hundredths**	Yes No	

Teacher Notes:
Representing Decimals

Questions to Consider About the Key Mathematical Concepts

Do students understand that a decimal fraction (often shortened to *decimal*) is another way of expressing a fraction, and that decimals, like fractions, can be represented in a variety of ways? To what extent, do they

- interpret visual representations of decimal fractions?
- apply an understanding of place value and the operation of addition to identify equivalent expressions?

Common Core Connection (4.NF.C.6)

Grade: Fourth

Domain: Number and Operations–Fractions

Cluster:

C. Understand decimal notation for fractions, and compare decimal fractions.

4.NF.C.6. Use decimal notation for fractions with denominators 10 or 100. For example, rewrite 0.62 as $\frac{62}{100}$; describe a length as 0.62 meters; locate 0.62 on a number line diagram.

Uncovering Student Understanding About the Key Concepts

Using the Representing Decimals Probe can provide the following information about how students are thinking about decimal fractions as numbers and how they relate to fractions.

Do they

- apply an understanding that decimals can be decomposed using place value?

OR

Do they

- lack conceptual understanding of how the location of a digit provides information about its size?

Do they

- express decimals as equivalent fractions?

OR

- express decimals with visual representations such as number lines and area model?

OR

Do they

- lack understanding of the relationship of fractions and decimals and think about them as completely separate ideas?

- have difficulty interpreting how visual and numeric representations relate?

*E*xploring Excerpts From Educational Resources and Related Research

Common areas of difficulty for students:

Data from the Mathematics Assessment for Learning and Teaching (MaLT) project data base indicate that students demonstrate the following types of difficulty understanding equivalence of fractions and decimals. They have difficulties using place value to name a decimal as a fraction and interpreting decimal notation. For example, 12% of students expressed $\frac{2}{100}$ as .2 or 2. (Ryan & Williams, 2007, pp. 212, 214)

Students sometimes misapply the methods of reading whole-number place value names to reading decimals. For example, they think that because hundreds are the third whole-number place, hundredths should also be the third place in decimals. (Bay Area Mathematics Task Force, 1999, p. 74)

Students and teachers have found learning and teaching place value difficult. This difficulty is related to the complexity of our numeration system. Understanding place value requires understanding a variety of mathematical properties including the additive, positional, base-ten and multiplicative properties. (Ross, 2002, p 419)

*S*urveying the Prompts and Selected Responses in the Probe

The justified list Probe consists of six selected response items, each related to a common prompt. The Probe is designed to assess understanding of equivalent decimal representations. The prompts and selected responses are designed to elicit understandings and common difficulties as described in the following table:

If a student chooses	*It is likely that the student*
C, D and F: Yes A, B, and E: No (correct responses)	• is able to decompose a decimal using place value and express the decomposed decimal in fractional form. • uses place value to visually represent a decimal to the hundredths place [See Sample Student Response 1]. *Look for indication of the student's understanding in the written explanations of how the student got the answer.*
A; Yes and/or D or F: No	• has difficulty decomposing a decimal or is confused about place value [See Sample Student Response 2].
B: Yes C: No	• has difficulty interpreting visual representations of decimals [See Sample Student Response 3]. • has difficulty reasoning about the size of a decimal in relation to other decimals.
E: Yes	• has difficulty interpreting the meaning of the decimal point and expressing decimals as fractions [See Sample Student Response 4].

Teaching Implications and Considerations

Ideas for eliciting more information from students about their understanding and difficulties:

- For students who answer the prompts correctly but whose explanations are not clear or complete, ask for clarification of explanations to ensure understanding. Listen for evidence of understanding of place value and decimal–fraction equivalence.
- For students with errors, ask questions to learn about their approach:
  - How do you read this number (0.43)?
  - How did you decide which visual representations showed 0.43?
  - Select a response that is not equivalent and ask, "Why do you think someone might choose this incorrect response?"

Ideas for planning instruction in response to what you learned from the results of administering the Probe:

- Use a variety of concrete models and representations such as base-ten blocks, hundredths grids and disks, and number lines to develop conceptual understanding of decimals and their relationship to fractions.
- Reinforce the concept of the denominator of a decimal and the meaning of the decimal point by reading 3.72 as "three and seventy-two hundredths" rather than as "three point seven two" or "three point seventy-two." The latter translations can reinforce misconceptions related to applying whole number thinking to decimals.

- Write decimals with a leading zero in order to build understanding of the decimal point as a cue about the denominator. "Students can write '0. — — —' in preparation for writing 'five thousandths.' Because decimal denominators are not seen but are inferred from the number places, this method draws attention to the denominator" (Bay Area Mathematics Task Force, 1999, p. 75).

Sample Student Responses to Representing Decimals?

Responses That Suggest Understanding

Sample Student Response 1

The student chose "Yes" on Problem F and wrote, "13 hundredths is 1 tenth and 3 hundredths because I am thinking of regrouping with the blocks we used. 3 tenths and 1 tenths is 4 tenths just like the number says."

Responses That Suggest Difficulty

Sample Student Response 2

Student chose "No" on Problem A and wrote, "The numbers add up to 0.7. That's not 0.43."

Sample Student Response 3

Student chose "Yes" on Problem B and wrote, "It's three lines after the 0.4."

Sample Student Response 4

Student chose "Yes" on Problem E and wrote, "The / is like the decimal point so $\frac{4}{3}$ is 4.3."

Comparing to $\frac{1}{2}$

	Check one:	Explain your answer:
A. $\frac{1}{8}$	☐ Less than $\frac{1}{2}$ ☐ Greater than $\frac{1}{2}$ ☐ Equivalent to $\frac{1}{2}$	
B. $\frac{24}{42}$	☐ Less than $\frac{1}{2}$ ☐ Greater than $\frac{1}{2}$ ☐ Equivalent to $\frac{1}{2}$	
C. $\frac{6}{11}$	☐ Less than $\frac{1}{2}$ ☐ Greater than $\frac{1}{2}$ ☐ Equivalent to $\frac{1}{2}$	
D. $\frac{7}{14}$	☐ Less than $\frac{1}{2}$ ☐ Greater than $\frac{1}{2}$ ☐ Equivalent to $\frac{1}{2}$	
E. $\frac{3}{9}$	☐ Less than $\frac{1}{2}$ ☐ Greater than $\frac{1}{2}$ ☐ Equivalent to $\frac{1}{2}$	

Teacher Notes: Comparing to $\frac{1}{2}$

Questions to Consider About the Key Mathematical Concepts

Do students understand that a fraction is a number, and are they able to reason about the size of a fraction in comparison to $\frac{1}{2}$? To what extent, do they

- demonstrate an understanding of a fraction as a number whose numerator and denominator determine its value?
- explain how to compare fractions to a benchmark or landmark fraction?

Common Core Connection (4.NF)

Grade: Fourth

Domain: Number and Operations—Fractions

Cluster:

A. Extend understanding of fraction equivalence and ordering.

4.NF.A.2. Compare two fractions with different numerators and different denominators, e.g., by creating common denominators or numerators, or by comparing to a benchmark fraction such as $\frac{1}{2}$. Recognize that comparisons are valid only when the two fractions refer to the same whole. Record the results of comparisons with symbols >, =, or <, and justify the conclusions, e.g., by using a visual fraction model.

Uncovering Student Understanding About the Key Concepts

Using the Comparing to $\frac{1}{2}$ Probe can provide the following information about how students are thinking about fractions and their value.

Do they
- use multiplicative relationships between the numerators and denominators of fractions to reason about the fraction's proximity to landmarks such as 0, $\frac{1}{2}$, and 1?

OR

Do they
- apply whole number thinking to estimate the size of fractions or rely on computational procedures to compare fractions?

- write explanations that show conceptual understanding of the relative size of fractions?

OR

- write explanations that only show procedures such as cross multiplication or finding a common denominator?

Exploring Excerpts From Educational Resources and Related Research

Common areas of difficulty for students:

The words *more* and *greater* [italics in original] can lead to misunderstandings. More can mean more pieces in the partitioned whole, or more can mean more area covered by each part. Greater can mean a greater number of parts in the partitioned whole or a greater fraction size. . . . For example, many children responded that $\frac{1}{3}$ is greater than $\frac{1}{2}$ because you have more pieces when you divide the whole into thirds than when you divide the whole in halves. (Cramer, Post, & del Mas, 2002, p. 131)

Learning Pitfall: Applying whole number knowledge inappropriately to fractions. For example, students may look for one shaded out of two parts without understanding the need for congruent parts. (Bay Area Mathematics Task Force, 1999, p. 64)

Surveying the Prompts and Selected Responses in the Probe

The Probe consists of five selected response prompts and explanations designed to assess understanding of comparing fractions. The prompts and selected responses are designed to elicit understandings and common difficulties as described below.

If a student chooses	It is likely that the student
A, E: Less than B, C: Greater than D: Equivalent to (correct responses)	• applies understanding of the size of the pieces and the number of pieces to reason about how the size of a fraction compares to $\frac{1}{2}$. • performs procedures such as using common denominators to find equivalent fractions and compare fractions [See Sample Student Response 1]. *Look for indication of the student's understanding in the written explanations of how the student got the answer.*
All: Greater than	• may be applying whole number thinking to compare fractions (e.g. denominators are all larger than 2, difference between numerators and denominators greater than the difference between 2 and 1 in $\frac{1}{2}$) [See Sample Student Responses 2 and 3].

If a student chooses	It is likely that the student
B, C: Equivalent or Less than	• has difficulty reasoning about less common fractions that are close to $\frac{1}{2}$ but not equivalent to $\frac{1}{2}$ [See Sample Student Response 4].

Teaching Implications and Considerations

Ideas for eliciting more information from students about their understanding and difficulties:

- What do you look for and think about when you are trying to compare a fraction to $\frac{1}{2}$?
- How did you know how the fraction compared to $\frac{1}{2}$?
- Were some of these fractions easier for you to compare to $\frac{1}{2}$ than others?

Ideas for planning instruction in response to what you learned from the results of administering the Probe:

- Use concrete materials such as fraction circles, tiles, and visuals to build mental images of the size of a fraction and conceptual understanding the numerator and denominator.
- Use multiple representations such as area and number line models to build an understanding of fractions as numbers with a specific size that extend and provide more flexibility to our whole number system.
- "Build on students' informal understanding of sharing and proportionality to develop initial fraction concepts. Use equal-sharing activities to introduce the concept of fractions. Use sharing activities that involve dividing sets of objects as well as single whole objects. Extend equal-sharing activities to develop students' understanding of ordering and equivalence of fractions." (Siegler et al., 2010, p. 1)

Sample Student Responses to Comparing to $\frac{1}{2}$

Responses That Suggest Understanding

Sample Student Response 1

Student chose "Less than $\frac{1}{2}$" on Problem B and wrote, "$\frac{1}{2}$ means that the bottom number is always double the top number. 24 doubled is 48 not 42. 42 is less than 48 so that means $\frac{24}{42}$ is more than $\frac{1}{2}$ not less than half or = to $\frac{1}{2}$."

(Continued)

(Continued)

Responses That Suggest Difficulty

Sample Student Response 2

Student chose "Greater than $\frac{1}{2}$" on Problem C and wrote, "6 is greater than 1 and 11 is greater than 2."

Sample Student Response 3

Student chose "Greater than $\frac{1}{2}$" on Problem E and wrote, "I drew a picture and counted."

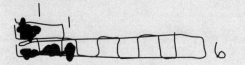

Variation: Comparing to $\frac{1}{2}$

Circle **ALL** of the numbers below that are greater than $\frac{1}{2}$

a. **0.45**

d. $\frac{2}{9}$

g. $\frac{4}{9}$

b. $\frac{5}{10}$

e. $\frac{7}{13}$

h. **0.6**

c. **0.07**

f. **0.50**

i. $\frac{1}{5}$

Explain how you decided whether or not to circle the number.

Fraction Estimates: Addition

Estimate without calculating. Circle the best estimate:	Explain your thinking:
1. $\dfrac{2}{3} + \dfrac{1}{2}$ a. More than 1 b. Less than 1	
2. $\dfrac{7}{8} + \dfrac{3}{4}$ a. More than 1 b. Less than 1	
3. $\dfrac{1}{8} + \dfrac{1}{6}$ a. More than $\dfrac{1}{2}$ b. Less than $\dfrac{1}{2}$	

Teacher Notes: Fraction Estimates: Addition

Questions to Consider About the Key Mathematical Concepts

When solving problems involving estimation of the addition of two fractions, can students reason about the size of the numbers and the effect of the operation? To what extent do they

- make sense of size of the fractions involved in the problem?
- make sense of the effect of combining the fractions?
- describe how to use this information to determine a reasonable estimation?

Common Core Connection (5.NF)

Grade: Fourth

Domain: Number and Operations—Fractions

Cluster:

B. Build fractions from unit fractions.

4.NF.B.3. Understand a fraction $\frac{a}{b}$ with $a > 1$ as a sum of fractions $\frac{1}{b}$.

4.NF.B.3a. Understand addition and subtraction of fractions as joining and separating parts referring to the same whole.

Uncovering Student Understanding About the Key Concepts

Using the Fraction Estimates: Addition Probe can provide the following information about how students are thinking about the effect of combining fractions.

Do they
- reason correctly about the size of the numbers?
- reason about the size of the product?

OR

OR

Do they
- apply incorrect benchmarking strategies?
- apply an overgeneralization of "multiplication always results in a bigger answer"?

Do they		*Do they*
• use reasoning to determine whether the sum is greater or less than a given benchmark?	OR	• use an algorithm to determine an exact answer to compare the given benchmark?

Exploring Excerpts From Educational Resources and Related Research

Common areas of difficulty for students:

Errors show that many students have learned rules for manipulating symbols without understanding what those symbols mean or why the rules work. Many students are unable to reason appropriately about symbols for rational numbers and do not have the strategic competence that would allow them to catch their mistakes. (NRC, 2001, p. 234)

Developing fluency requires a balance and connection between conceptual understanding and computational proficiency. Computational methods that are overpracticed without understanding are often forgotten or remembered incorrectly (Hiebert 1999; Kamii, Lewis, and Livingston 1993; Hiebert and Lindquist 1990). (NCTM, 2000, p. 35)

[Research has identified the following common roadblock for students related to estimation.] *When encouraged to estimate a solution, students still focus on solving the problem via a computational algorithm rather than estimating it.* [The same research suggests the following approach.] Estimation should be presented as a tool for anticipating the size and assessing the reasonableness of an answer. Teachers should focus on the reasoning needed to estimate a solution and should emphasize that estimation is a preliminary step to solving a problem, not a shortcut to obtaining an exact answer. Teachers who pose problems that cannot be solved quickly with mental computation (e.g., problems such as 5/9 + 3/7 rather than 5/8 + 3/8) will likely avoid this roadblock. (Siegler et al., 2010, p. 34)

Surveying the Prompts and Selected Responses in the Probe

The Probe consists of three selected response items, each with two choices. The prompts and selected responses are designed to elicit understandings and common difficulties as described in the following table:

If a student chooses	It is likely that the student
1. a. More than 1 2. a. More than 1 3. b. Less than $\frac{1}{2}$ (correct answer)	• correctly reasons about the size of the fractions and the effect of the operation; or • correctly applies an algorithm rather than using reasoning to determine an estimate [See Sample Student Response 1]. *Look for indication of the student's understanding in the written explanations of how the student got the answer.*

Other combinations	• applies one or more of the following incorrect approaches:
	
	  ○ adds the numerators and denominators and comparing the resulting fraction. For example, $\frac{2}{3}+\frac{1}{2}=\frac{3}{5}$ and $\frac{3}{5}$ is less than 1 [See Sample Student Response 2]; or
	  ○ incorrectly reasons about the size of one or both of the fractions. For example, viewing $\frac{1}{8}$ and $\frac{1}{6}$ as close to 1 since 8 and 6 are "big" numbers [See Sample Student Response 3]; or
	  ○ applies an algorithm incorrectly and compares the result [See Sample Student Response 4].

Teaching Implications and Considerations

Ideas for eliciting more information from students about their understanding and difficulties:

- For students who incorrectly reason about the size of the fractions or add the numerators and denominators, ask

  ○ "Can you create a model for each of these fractions?"
  ○ "How can this model help you determine whether the sum will be more or less than 1?"
- For students who apply an algorithm rather than estimating, ask, "How might you think about this without actually calculating an answer?"

Ideas for planning instruction in response to what you learned from the results of administering the Probe:

- Use representations and concrete models such as number lines and area models to help students understand the size of fractions.
- Focus on the meaning of the operation before introducing steps of an algorithm.
- Continue to require students to reason about the size of the numbers and the effect of the operation to determine an estimate as a method of checking for the reasonableness of the results of applying an algorithm.

Sample Student Responses to Fraction Estimates: Addition

Responses That Suggest Understanding

Sample Student Response 1

Student chose "Less than $\frac{1}{2}$" on Problem 3 and wrote, "Both $\frac{1}{8}$ and $\frac{1}{6}$ are less than $\frac{1}{4}$ so it has to be less than $\frac{1}{2}$ together. It takes $\frac{1}{4}$ and $\frac{1}{4}$ to get to $\frac{1}{2}$."

Responses That Suggest Difficulty

Sample Student Response 2

Student chose "Less than 1" on Problem 2 and wrote, "7 + 3 = 10 and 8 + 4 = 12 so it's $\frac{10}{12}$. 10 is less than 12 so $\frac{10}{12}$ is less than whole."

Sample Student Response 3

Student chose "More than $\frac{1}{2}$" on Problem 3 and wrote, "Both $\frac{1}{8}$ and $\frac{1}{6}$ are bigger than $\frac{1}{2}$ so putting together would be more than $\frac{1}{2}$."

Sample Student Response 4

Student chose "Less than 1" on Problem 2 and wrote, "$\frac{3}{4}$ is $\frac{6}{8}$. $\frac{7}{8}$ and $\frac{6}{8}$ is $\frac{13}{16}$."

4.5V

Variation: Fraction Estimates: Subtraction

Estimate the difference without calculating. Circle the best estimate:	Explain your thinking:
1. $\dfrac{6}{7} - \dfrac{5}{6}$ a. More than $\dfrac{1}{2}$ b. Less than $\dfrac{1}{2}$	
2. $\dfrac{10}{8} - \dfrac{2}{7}$ a. More than $\dfrac{1}{2}$ b. Less than $\dfrac{1}{2}$	
3. $\dfrac{3}{4} - \dfrac{3}{13}$ a. More than $\dfrac{1}{2}$ b. Less than $\dfrac{1}{2}$	

5

Measurement and Data Probes

The content of the Probes in this chapter aligns with the standards for Grades 3 through 5. The Probes and their variations will also be relevant beyond the aligned grade level for students in higher grades who have not yet met standards from previous grade levels as well as for students who have already met the standards at their own grade level.

We developed these Probes to address the following critical areas of focus, described in the standards (CCSSO, 2010):

- Represent and interpret data.
- Solve problems involving measurement and conversion of measurements from a larger unit to a smaller unit.
- Convert like measurement units within a given measurement system.
- Geometric measurement: understand concepts of area and relate area to multiplication and to addition.
- Geometric measurement: recognize perimeter as an attribute of plane figures and distinguish between linear and area measures.
- Geometric measurement: understand concepts of volume and relate volume to multiplication and to addition.

The content of the Probes in this chapter aligns with the standards for Grades 3 through 5. The Probes and their variations will also be relevant beyond the aligned grade level for students in higher grades who have not yet met standards from previous grade levels as well as for students who have already met the standards at their own grade level.

Common Core Math Content

Common Core Mathematical Content	Related Question	Probe Name
Solve one- and two-step "how many more" and "how many less" problems using information presented in scaled bar graphs 3.MD.B.3	Are students able to interpret the information represented in frequency bar graphs in order to answer questions about the data?	What Does the Graph Say? (p. 130)
Generate measurement data by measuring lengths using rulers marked with halves and fourths of an inch. 3.MD.B.4 Note: The Probe addresses the foundation concept of measuring lengths.	Do students understand that the length of an object is the number of same-size length units that span the object? Do they also understand that units of length can be further partitioned to provide a more accurate measure?	Comparing Lengths (p. 135) Variation: Determining the Length of the Rope (p. 140)
Know relative sizes of measurement units within one system of units including km, m, cm; kg, g; lb, oz; l, ml; hr, min, sec. Within a single system of measurement, express measurements in a larger unit in terms of a smaller unit. 4.MD.A.1	Do students understand the relationship between units within one system of measurement?	Estimating Measures (p. 142) Variation: Comparing Units of Measure (p. 147)
Convert among different-size standard measurement units within a given measurement system. 5.MD.A.1	Do students understand the relationship between units within the metric measuring system?	Comparing Metric Measures (p. 148)

Remember to take a look at the variations that are available with some of the Probes in this chapter. All of these variations address measurement and data but may extend the idea or offer a different structure for administering them. When available, variation Probes follow the Teacher Notes and associated reproducibles for the related original Probe.

What Does the Graph Say?

During lunch, Emma asked some students to choose one favorite color; then she created a bar chart using the data.

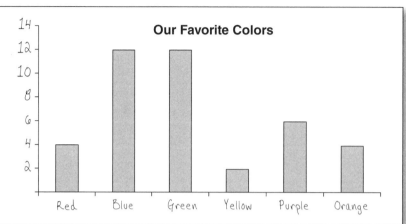

Decide if the statement is true or false.	Circle True or False:	Explain your thinking:
A. Four more students chose **blue** than chose **red.**	True False	
B. The numbers of students who chose **blue** is four more than the number who chose **red** and **orange** combined.	True False	
C. Twenty students answered the question.	True False	
D. Twice as many students chose **purple** as chose **yellow.**	True False	
E. More than half of the students chose either **blue** or **purple.**	True False	
F. Twice as many students chose **red** as chose **yellow.**	True False	

Teacher Notes:
What Does the Graph Say?

Questions to Consider About the Key Mathematical Concepts

Are students able to interpret the information represented in frequency bar graphs in order to answer questions about the data? To what extent do they

- understand the importance of determining the scale factor?
- use the scale factor and height of the bar to determine the frequency of a particular category of data?
- accurately solve numeric comparisons between two or more categories?

Common Core Connection (3.MD)

Grade: Third

Domain: Measurement and Data

Cluster:

B. Represent and interpret data.

3.MD.B.3. Draw a scaled picture graph and a scaled bar graph to represent a data set with several categories. Solve one- and two-step "how many more" and "how many less" problems using information presented in scaled bar graphs.

Uncovering Student Understanding About the Key Concepts

Using the What Does the Graph Say? Probe can provide the following information about how students are thinking about interpreting graphs.

Do they

- correspond the value of each bar with the number in the scale to determine the numbers in the data set?

OR

- interpret the data set to answer questions?

Do they

- use a scale factor of one?

OR

- have difficulty interpreting the questions?

Exploring Excerpts From Educational Resources and Related Research

Common areas of difficulty for students:

[Data from the Mathematics Assessment for Learning and Teaching (MaLT) project indicate that students have difficulty with recognizing and interpreting graphs.] Errors were found that involved children ignoring terms like "more" or "less" in a task. Thus children would correctly answer "How many did Kate get?" but incorrectly answer, "How many more did John get than Fred?" (Ryan & Williams, 2007, p. 121)

Students' conceptual ability to analyze data and draw conclusions and interpretations is often weak (Tarr & Shaughnessy, 2007), so work on emphasizing this higher-level skill will support the development of statistical thinking. (Van de Walle et al., 2013, p. 442)

A new view of mathematical representations in general and graphing in particular has slowly emerged in the past decade. Instead of being isolated curricular items to be taught and tested as ends in themselves, graphs along with diagrams, charts, number sentences, and formulas, are increasingly seen as useful tools for building understanding and for communicating both information and understanding. (NCTM, 2003, p. 250)

Surveying the Prompts and Selected Responses in the Probe

The justified list Probe consists of one prompt and six true–false selected responses. The prompts and selected responses are designed to elicit understandings and common difficulties as described below.

If a student chooses	*It is likely that the student*
A. False B. True C. False D. False E. False F. True (correct responses)	• is able to interpret the scale on the bar graph to answer a variety of category comparison questions [See Sample Student Responses 1 and 2]. *Look for indication of the student's understanding in the written explanations of how the student got the answer.*

A. True
B. False
C. True
D. True
E. True
F. False
	• is applying one or more of the following errors:
	
	  ○ disregarding the scale factor of 2 (viewing each interval as one student rather than two students); [See Sample Student Response 3].
	  ○ difficulty with more than, less than, and twice as many comparisons [See Sample Student Response 4].

Teaching Implications and Considerations

Ideas for eliciting more information from students about their understanding and difficulties:

- To learn more about what the student understands about interpreting a graph, ask, "What do each of the bars represent in the graph? What do these numbers on the side mean?"
- For students with correct and incorrect answers, ask questions to learn more about their interpretation of the task as well as their approach: "What is this problem about? Can you explain to me what you did to decide on this particular answer choice?"

Ideas for planning instruction in response to what you learned from the results of administering the Probe:

- Provide opportunities for students to represent data they have collected using a variety of scale factors. Discuss how the data look similar and different based on the scale choice.
- Have students verbalize what the horizontal and vertical axes represent on various graphs.
- Allow students to create their own questions or true–false statements related to the graphed data.
- When posing questions about the data, be sure to include those that require students to compare across two or more categories answering "more than" or "less than" questions.
- Have students analyze a variety of graphs that were created by other sources: students, newspapers, the Internet, and so on.

Sample Student Responses to What Does the Graph Say?

Responses That Suggest Understanding

Sample Student Response 1

Student chose "False" for Problem A, and wrote, "I think it's false because red is 4 people and blue is 12 people, so this is 8 more people choosing blue."

Sample Student Response 2

Student chose "False" for Problem C, and wrote, "4 + 12 + 12 + 2 + 6 + 4 = 40 people."

Responses That Suggest Difficulty

Sample Student Response 3

Student chose "False" for Problem A and wrote, "No, it is 10 because 12 − 2 is 10."

(Continued)

(Continued)

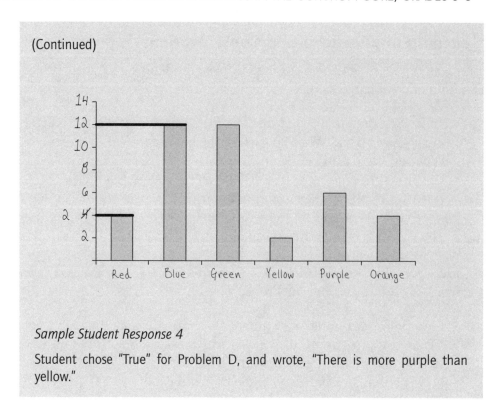

Sample Student Response 4

Student chose "True" for Problem D, and wrote, "There is more purple than yellow."

Comparing Lengths

About how much longer is the marker than the pencil?	Choose one:	Explain your answer:
1.	a. $\frac{1}{4}$ unit b. $\frac{1}{2}$ unit c. $\frac{3}{4}$ unit d. 1 unit	
2.	a. They are the same length. b. $\frac{1}{4}$ unit c. 1 unit d. $1\frac{1}{4}$ unit	
3.	a. $\frac{1}{4}$ unit b. $\frac{1}{2}$ unit c. 1 unit d. $1\frac{1}{4}$ unit	

Teacher Notes: Comparing Lengths

Questions to Consider About the Key Mathematical Concepts

Do students understand that the length of an object is the number of same-size length units that span the object? Do they also understand that units of length can be further partitioned to provide a more accurate measure? To what extent, do they

- determine the measure of an object using whole length units and parts of the whole length unit (partitions of one-half and one-fourth)?
- consider a non-zero starting point when measuring the length of an object?
- accurately compare the length of two objects using the same-size length unit?

Common Core Connection (3.MD.B.4)

Grade: Third

Domain: Measurement and Data

Cluster:

B. Represent and interpret data.

3.MD.B.4. Generate measurement data by measuring lengths using rulers marked with halves and fourths of an inch.

Note: The Probe addresses the foundation concept of measuring lengths.

Uncovering Student Understanding About the Key Concepts

Using the Comparing Lengths Probe can provide the following information about how students are thinking about finding and comparing length measures to the nearest one-fourth unit.

Do they

- consider the alignment of the object to the start and end points of objects and measurement tools?

OR

Do they

- ignore the start and determine the difference in length based only on the end point of the objects?

Do they		*Do they*
• understand that the difference in the length is how many units longer one object (marker) is than the other object (pencil)?	OR	• count hash marks rather than intervals to determine the difference?

*E*xploring Excerpts From Educational Resources and Related Research

Common areas of difficulty for students:

Children's understanding of zero-point is particularly tenuous. Only a minority of young children understand that any point on a scale can serve as the starting point, and even a significant minority of older children (e.g., fifth grade) respond to non-zero origins by simply reading off whatever number on a ruler aligns with the end of the object (Lehrer et al., 1998a). Many children throughout schooling begin measuring with one rather than zero. (Ellis, Siegler, & Van Voorhis, 2001) (NCTM, 2003, p. 183)

Conceptual understanding of measurement includes, among others, understanding of iteration and understanding of the origin. Specific ideas include (1) the need for identical units; (2) partitioning of a unit; (3) conformity on the scale [meaning] that any location on the scale can serve as the origin; (4) mental coordination of the origin and the endpoint of the scale and the resulting measure. Most studies suggest that these understandings of units of length are acquired over the course of the elementary grades. (NCTM, 2003, p. 182)

Children may have difficulty identifying the relation between the numeral that labels the measure and the process of measuring that gives rise to it. Thus the label 5 on the ruler indicates that there are 5 units of length that can be counted "up to that point" from an origin on the ruler (labeled zero). Note that these 5 units are intervals between numerals, and that there are 6 numerals involved in the process of measuring a length of 5 units. Lack of awareness or understanding of this relation may explain many errors with numerals and scales when measuring or even when counting on the number line. (Ryan & Williams, 2007, p. 26)

Surveying the Prompts and Selected Responses in the Probe

The Probe consists of three selected response items, each with four choices. The prompts and selected responses are designed to elicit understandings and common difficulties as described below.

If a student chooses	It is likely that the student
1. c 2. c 3. d (correct responses)	• is viewing the length as the number of whole and partitioned units from the beginning to the end of the object. • is able to compare the lengths of the two objects [See Sample Student Response 1]. *Look for indication of the student's understanding in the written explanations of how the student got the answer.*
2. a 3. b	• is comparing the endpoints of the objects without considering the different starting points [See Sample Student Response 2].
3. c	• is comparing the starting point of the objects without considering the different endpoints [See Sample Student Response 3].
Various other choices	• is having difficulty with measures that are partitioned into quarters [See Sample Student Response 4].

Teaching Implications and Considerations

Ideas for eliciting more information from students about their understanding and difficulties:

- How long is the marker? The ruler?
- How did you determine the difference in the lengths?
- What do these hash marks between the long labeled hash marks numbers mean?

Ideas for planning instruction in response to what you learned from the results of administering the Probe:

- Have students construct their own rulers, marking the units and partitioning the units into various sized intervals.
- When using conventional tools such as rulers and tape measures for measuring length, provide explicit instruction. For example, help them learn to interpret the markings on a ruler, the different units to choose from, and where the "0," or beginning point, is located. (NCTM, 2000, p. 173)

- Connect units of measure on rulers to number line concepts such as endpoints, hash marks and intervals and finding the distance between two points.
- Provide experience with a variety of standard and nonstandard measuring tools with varying intervals and units.
- Offering opportunities to measure length with "broken rulers" can help students learn to compensate for a nonzero starting point.

Sample Student Responses to Comparing Lengths

Responses That Suggest Understanding

Sample Student Response 1

Student chose "c. $\frac{3}{4}$ unit" for Problem 1 and wrote, "The marker is $4\frac{3}{4}$ units long and the pencil is 4 units long so the difference is $\frac{3}{4}$ unit."

Responses That Suggest Difficulty

Sample Student Response 2

Student chose "a. They are the same length" for Problem 2 and wrote, "These are the same because both go to the same spot on the ruler."

Sample Student Response 3

Student chose "b. $\frac{1}{2}$ unit" for Problem 3 and wrote, "I think it's $\frac{1}{2}$ because the pencil goes to 5 and the marker goes to $5\frac{1}{2}$."

Variation: Determining the Length of the Rope

Susie is using minicrayons to measure different-size pieces of rope. The pieces of rope and minicrayons are shown below.

Problems 1–3

Decide if each piece of Susie's rope is 3 minicrayons long.	Circle one:
1	Yes No
2	Yes No
3	Yes No

Explain how you decided whether to circle Yes or No:

Problems 4–6

Decide if each piece of Susie's rope is 3 minicrayons long.		Circle one:
4		Yes No
5		Yes No
6		Yes No

Explain how you decided whether to circle Yes or No:

Estimating Measures

Circle the best estimate.	Explain your choice:
1. Susie has a pencil that is 6 inches long. She is using the pencil to measure the length of a table in her classroom. If the length of the table is 14 pencils, which is the best estimate of the length of the table in feet? a. 7 ft b. 14 ft c. 28 ft	
2. Eric is using a broomstick that is 2 meters long to measure the length of the classroom. If the length of the classroom is 5 broomsticks, which is the best estimate of the length of the classroom in centimeters? a. 100 cm b. 10 cm c. 1,000 cm	

Teacher Notes: Estimating Measures

Questions to Consider About the Key Mathematical Concepts

Do students understand the relationship between units within one system of measurement? To what extent, do they

- understand the inverse relationship between the size of the unit of measure and the number of units?
- use unit equivalence to express lengths in units within the same system?
- use information about measurement in nonstandard units to solve problems involving measurement with standard units?

Common Core Connection (4.MD)

Grade: Fourth

Domain: Measurement and Data

Cluster:

A. Solve problems involving measurement and conversion of measurements from a larger unit to a smaller unit.

4.MD.A.1. Know relative sizes of measurement units within one system of units including km, m, cm; kg, g; lb, oz; l, ml; hr, min, sec. Within a single system of measurement, express measurements in a larger unit in terms of a smaller unit.

Uncovering Student Understanding About the Key Concepts

Using the Estimating Measures Probe can provide the following information about how students are thinking about the relationship between nonstandard and standard measures and units within the same measurement system.

Do they
- apply understanding of the relationship between units of measure—when a length is measured with a unit of measure that is larger, the number of units will be less than when that object is measured with a smaller unit of measure?

OR

Do they
- have difficulty seeing the relationship between the size of the unit and number of units?

Do they

- apply understanding of standard units of measure and measurement conversion to solve problems involving nonstandard units of measure?

OR

Do they

- have difficulty applying reasoning about measurement with nonstandard objects to making a standard measurement?

- lack knowledge of measurement equivalents (inches and feet and meters and centimeters)?

Exploring Excerpts From Educational Resources and Related Research

Common areas of difficulty for students:

Measures of distances requires restructuring space so that one "sees" counts of units as representing an iteration of successive distances. Iteration refers to accumulating units of measure to obtain a quantity, such as 12 inches. It rests on a foundation of sub-dividing length and ordering the subdivisions (Piaget et al., 1960). Thus, a count of n units represents a distance of n units . . . the construction of unit involves a web of foundational ideas including procedures of iteration, recognition of the need for identical units, understanding of the inverse relationship between magnitude of each unit and the resulting length measure, and understanding partitions of unit. (NCTM, 2003, p. 182)

[Students] overgeneralize what they know about place value and renaming when solving problems that involve renaming measurement units (for example, applying what they know about tens when renaming feet to inches or hours to minutes). (Bamberger, Oberdorf, & Schultz-Farrell, 2010, p. 134)

The relationships between units within either the metric or customary system are conventions. As such, students must simply be told what the relationships are, and instructional activities must be devised to reinforce them. (Van de Walle et al., 2013, p. 379)

Surveying the Prompts and Selected Responses in the Probe

The Probe consists of two selected response items, each with three choices. The prompts and selected responses are designed to elicit understandings and common difficulties as described in the following table:

If a student chooses	It is likely that the student
1. a 2. c (correct responses)	• is correctly applying unit equivalencies to express measurements in units within the same system • applies reasoning about nonstandard measurement to derive a standard measurement; check their explanation for indications of conversion reasoning [See Sample Student Response 1]. *Look for indication of the student's understanding in the written explanations of how the student got the answer.*
1. c 2. a	• incorrectly reasons about the relationship of the related units of measure or incorrectly converts from one unit to another [See Sample Student Response 2].
1. b 2. b	• draws on information given in the problem without considering the comparison of the lengths and the context of the problem; or • draws on information given in the problem but performs computation that does not make sense for the context or incorrectly converts between units of measure [See Sample Student Response 3].

Teaching Implications and Considerations

Ideas for eliciting more information from students about their understanding and difficulties:

- How did you decide upon your choice?
- How is it possible that they have measured with objects like pencils and broomsticks and are able to get measurements in standard units of measure like inches and centimeters?
- How do inches and feet compare? How do centimeters and meters compare?
- Are you able to make a picture or visual to represent the problem?

Ideas for planning instruction in response to what you learned from the results of administering the Probe:

- Provide opportunities for students to develop mental images and benchmarks of common items and their relationship to standard units of measure.
- Provide opportunities to compare and estimate lengths. For example, "This object is about three times the length of this object." "This object is about a foot longer than this object." "This object is about three meters in length."
- Connect metric conversation to decimal place value concepts.
- Provide multiple examples for students to understand the inverse relationship between the size of the units and the number of units needed.

Sample Student Responses to Estimating Measures

Responses That Suggest Understanding

Sample Student Response 1

Student chose "a. 7 ft" for the answer to Problem 1 and wrote, "Two pencils together are 12 inches or 1 foot. So, if there are 14 pencils, that would be 7 feet."

Responses That Suggest Difficulty

Sample Student Response 2

Student chose "c. 28 ft" on Problem 1 and wrote, "It takes 2 of something 6 inches long to make one foot, so you double the answer. 14 doubled is 28."

Sample Student Response 3

Student chose "b. 10 cm" for Problem 2 and wrote, "5 broomsticks and 2 meters long. 5 × 2 = 10."

Variation: Comparing Units of Measures

Circle one:			Explain your choice:
A. **12 inches**	More than Less than Same as	**1 foot**	
B. **12 hours**	More than Less than Same as	**2 days**	
C. **2 meters**	More than Less than Same as	**10 centimeters**	
D. **2 hours**	More than Less than Same as	**100 minutes**	

Comparing Metric Measures

Decide whether you agree or disagree with the statements below.	Explain your choice:
1. A cat weighs 500 g. A puppy weighs 2 kg. I think the cat weighs more than the puppy. Agree Disagree	
2. A raccoon is 0.8 m long. A baby fox is 67 cm long. I think the fox is longer than the raccoon. Agree Disagree	

Teacher Notes:
Comparing Metric Measures

Questions to Consider About the Key Mathematical Concepts

Do students understand the relationship between units within the metric measuring system? To what extent, do they

- use the power of 10 relationships and an understanding of metric units and equivalencies to move between metric measures?
- use place value reasoning to make indirect comparisons of sizes of measures with two different units?
- understand the difference between converting from a larger unit to a smaller unit and converting from a smaller unit to a larger unit?

Common Core Connection (5.MD)

Grade: Fifth

Domain: Measurement and Data

Cluster:

A. Convert like measurement units within a given measurement system.

5.MD.A.1. Convert among different-size standard measurement units within a given measurement system.

Uncovering Student Understanding About the Key Concepts

Using the Comparing Metric Measures Probe can provide the following information about how students are thinking about the relationship between metric measures.

Do they

- convert to a common unit of measure?

OR

Do they

- compare the numbers without first converting?
- rely on what they might know about the animals rather than the measures provided?

Do they

- apply place value understanding when converting?

OR

Do they

- convert in the wrong direction?

Exploring Excerpts From Educational Resources and Related Research

Common areas of difficulty for students:

Data from the Mathematics Assessment for Learning and Teaching (MaLT) project database indicate that students have difficulty with metric conversions such as converting between grams and kilogram. One difficulty identified was dividing or multiplying by 100 instead of 1000. (Ryan & Williams, 2007, p. 199)

The relationships between units within either the metric or customary system are conventions. As such, students must simply be told what the relationships are, and instructional activities must be devised to reinforce them. (Van de Walle et al., 2013, p. 379)

Surveying the Prompts and Selected Responses in the Probe

The Probe consists of two selected response items, each with two choices. The prompts and selected responses are designed to elicit understandings and common difficulties as described below.

If a student chooses	It is likely that the student
1. Disagree 2. Disagree (correct responses)	• is correctly comparing the different metric measures; check their explanation for indications of place value reasoning [See Sample Student Response 1]. *Look for indication of the student's understanding in the written explanations of how the student got the answer.*

1. Agree
2. Agree
	• student has one or more of the following difficulties:
	  ○ relying on his concept image of each of the animals rather than comparing the actual measures [See Sample Student Response 2]; or
	  ○ comparing the numbers without considering the size of the units [See Sample Student Response 3]; or
	  ○ lacking knowledge of relationship between metric units (i.e., 1 kg = 1,000g; 1 m = 100cm) [See Sample Student Response 4].

*T*eaching Implications and Considerations

Ideas for eliciting more information from students about their understanding and difficulties:

- How did you decide whether you agree or disagree?
- For students who rely on their mental images of the animals, ask questions such as,
  - ○ "Do you think all cats weigh more than all puppies?"
  - ○ "Can you explain, in general, how these two units of measures (kg and g or cm and m) compare?"
  - ○ "Can you express the weight/length of these animals using the same unit of measure?"

Ideas for planning instruction in response to what you learned from the results of administering the Probe:

- Provide opportunities for students to develop mental images and benchmarks related to metric units.
- Connect metric conversion to place value concepts and teach unit equivalencies.
- Provide multiple examples for students to understand the inverse relationship between the size of the units and the number of units needed.

Sample Student Responses to Comparing Metric Measures

Responses That Suggest Difficulty

Sample Student Response 1

Student chose "Disagree" for Problem 2 and wrote, ".8 m = .80 = 80 centimeters. 80 cm is longer than 67."

Responses That Suggest Understanding

Sample Student Response 2

Student chose "Disagree" for Problem 1 and wrote, "Because a dog depending on what kind you have it can grow bigger than a cat."

Sample Student Response 3

Student chose "Agree" for Problem 2 and wrote, "67 > 8, so the fox is longer."

Sample Student Response 4

Student chose "Agree" for Problem 1 and wrote, "Because I'm pretty sure that kilograms are half the size of a gram."

Geometry and Geometric Measurement Probes

The content of the Probes in this chapter aligns with the standards for Grades 3 through 5. The Probes and their variations will also be relevant beyond the aligned grade level for students in higher grades who have not yet met standards from previous grade levels as well as for students who have already met the standards at their own grade level.

We developed these Probes to address the following critical areas of focus, described in the standards (CCSSO, 2010):

> The content of the Probes in this chapter aligns with the standards for Grades 3 through 5. The Probes and their variations will also be relevant beyond the aligned grade level for students in higher grades who have not yet met standards from previous grade levels as well as for students who have already met the standards at their own grade level.

- Reason with shapes and their attributes.
- Classify two-dimensional figures into categories based on their properties.
- Draw and identify lines and angles, and classify shapes by properties of their lines and angles.

Remember to take a look at the variations that are available with some of the Probes in this chapter. All of these variations address geometric measurement and geometry ideas but may extend the idea or offer a different structure for administering them. When available, variation Probes follow the Teacher Notes and associated reproducibles for the related original Probe.

Common Core Math Content

Common Core Mathematical Content	Related Question	Probe Name
Relate area to the operations of multiplication and addition. 3.MD.C.7 Solve real-world and mathematical problems involving perimeters of polygons, including finding the perimeter given the side lengths, finding an unknown side length, and exhibiting rectangles with the same perimeter and different areas or with the same area and different perimeters. 3.MD.D.8	Do students understand area as a two-dimensional measure of the number of square units that fill a space without gaps or overlaps?	Finding Area (p. 154) Variation: Finding the Perimeter (p. 158)
Apply the area and perimeter formulas for rectangles in real-world and mathematical problems. For example, find the width of a rectangular room, given the area of the flooring and the length, by viewing the area formula as a multiplication equation with an unknown factor. 4.MD.A.3	Do students understand the meaning of perimeter and how to determine the perimeter of a rectangle, given its dimensions?	Naming the Perimeter (p. 159)
Apply the formulas $V = l \times w \times h$ and $V = b \times h$ for rectangular prisms to find volumes of right rectangular prisms with whole-number edge lengths in the context of solving real-world and mathematical problems. 5.MD.C.5b	When solving problems involving geometric measurement, can students determine the volume of a rectangular prism?	Volume of the Box (p. 164)
Classify two-dimensional figures based on the presence or absence of parallel or perpendicular lines, or the presence or absence of angles of a specified size. Recognize right triangles as a category, and identify right triangles. 4.G.A.2	Do students understand the concept of an angle and how to classify angles as right, obtuse, or acute, and how to describe angles within figures?	Classifying Angles Card Sort (p. 168) Variation: What's the Angle? (p. 176)
Understand that attributes belonging to a category of two-dimensional figures also belong to all subcategories of that category. For example, all rectangles have four right angles and squares are rectangles, so all squares have four right angles. 5.G.B.3 Classify two-dimensional figures in a hierarchy based on properties. 5.G.B.4	Do students understand the properties and characteristics of special types of quadrilaterals?	Names of the Shape (p. 178)

Finding Area

Four students are working together to find the area of the shaded rectangle.

Area = ?

I think the area is 35 square units.

Aisha

I think the area is 15 square units.

Juanita

I think the area is 16 square units.

Karl

I think the area is 20 square units.

Samson

Circle one: Aisha Juanita Karl Samson	Explain your choice. Include in your explanation why you disagree with the other students.

Teacher Notes:
Finding Area

Questions to Consider About the Key Mathematical Concepts

Do students understand area as a two-dimensional measure of the number of square units that fill a space without gaps or overlaps? To what extent, do they

- tile space inside a figure with unit squares in order to find the area of the figure?
- apply the formula A = length × width when finding area?
- distinguish between area and perimeter?
- make sense of given figures to determine the area of part of the figure?

Common Core Connection (3.MD)

Grade: Third

Domain: Measurement and Data

Clusters:

C. Geometric Measurement: Understand concepts of area and relate area to multiplication and to addition.

3.MD.C.7. Relate area to the operations of multiplication and addition.

D. Geometric Measurement: Recognize perimeter.

3.MD.D.8. Solve real-world and mathematical problems involving perimeters of polygons, including finding the perimeter given the side lengths, finding an unknown side length, and exhibiting rectangles with the same perimeter and different areas or with the same area and different perimeters.

Uncovering Student Understanding About the Key Concepts

Using the Finding Area Probe can provide the following information about how students are thinking about determining the area of a rectangular region.

Do they

- determine the length and width based on the information provided?

OR

- find the area by tiling or multiplying the length and the width?

OR

Do they

- include the corner squares when determining the length and/or width measures?

- determine the perimeter instead of the area?

Exploring Excerpts From Educational Resources and Related Research

Common areas of difficulty for students:

Area and perimeter are continually a source of confusion for students. Perhaps it is because both involve regions to be measured or because students are taught formulas for both concepts and tend to get the formulas confused. (Van de Walle, 2007, p. 386)

Children have problems with area and perimeter, and it is more than simply a question of remembering which is which! In our research we found that only 20 percent of 9-year-olds could correctly count the "distance round the outside of the shape." (Ryan & Williams, 2007, p. 101)

Surveying the Prompts and Selected Responses in the Probe

The Probe consists of one selected response item in a math-talk format. The prompts and selected responses are designed to elicit understandings and common difficulties as described below.

If a student chooses	It is likely that the student
Juanita (correct response)	• determines the area of the 5 × 3 shaded region [See Sample Student Response 1]. *Look for indication of the student's understanding in the written explanations of how the student got the answer.*
Aisha	• finds the area of the shaded rectangle *and* the border squares [See Sample Student Response 2].
Karl	• finds the perimeter of the shaded rectangle [See Sample Student Response 3].
Samson	• counts all of the square tiles around the shaded region [See Sample Student Response 4].

Teaching Implications and Considerations

Ideas for eliciting more information from students about their understanding and difficulties:

- Can you show me how you determined the area?
- How can you divide up this region in order to determine the area?
- How can the square units around the shaded region help you?

Ideas for planning instruction in response to what you learned from the results of administering the Probe:

- "Differentiating perimeter from area is facilitated by having students draw congruent rectangles and measure, mark off, and label the unit lengths all around the perimeter on one rectangle, then do the same on the other rectangle but also draw the square units. This enables students to see the units involved in length and area and find patterns in finding the lengths and areas of non-square and square rectangles." (Common Core State Standards Writing Team, 2012a, p. 18)

Sample Student Responses to Finding Area

Responses That Suggest Understanding

Sample Student Response 1

Student chose "Juanita," and wrote, "Area is length times width. I counted to find length. Length is 5 units. I counted to find width. Width is 3 units. Area is 5 × 3."

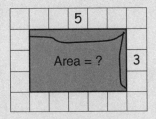

Responses That Suggest Difficulty

Sample Student Response 2

Student chose "Aisha," and wrote, "I think Aisha is right. Count over and down. 7 × 5 is 35."

Sample Student Response 3

Student chose "Karl," and wrote, "Karl went all the way around the shading."

Sample Student Response 4

Student chose "Samson," and wrote, "I agree with Samson because I counted all the squares."

Variation: Finding the Perimeter

6.1V

Circle **ALL** the shapes below that have the same **perimeter** as

a.

d.

b.

e.

c.

f.

Explain how you decided whether or not to circle the shape.

Naming the Perimeter

Look at the rectangle shown below:

4 units

7 units

Circle **ALL** of the expressions that could be used to find the **PERIMETER** of the rectangle above.

a. 4 × 7

b. 7 + 4

c. 11 × 2

d. 7 × 4 × 2

e. 2 × (4 + 7)

f. 7 + 4 + 7 + 4

g. 2 × 7 + 2 × 4

h. 4 + 7 × 2

Explain how you determined which expressions represent the perimeter and which do not.

Teacher Notes: Naming the Perimeter

Questions to Consider About the Key Mathematical Concepts

Do students understand the meaning of perimeter and how to determine the perimeter of a rectangle given its dimensions? To what extent, do they

- demonstrate an understanding that the perimeter is the distance around the outside of a two-dimensional shape?
- apply an understanding that unlabeled sides of a rectangle have the same lengths as the opposite side?
- identify equivalent expressions to express the perimeter?

Common Core Connection (4.MD)

Grade: Fourth

Domain: Measurement and Data

Cluster:

A. Solve problems involving measurement and conversion of measurements from a larger unit to a smaller unit.

4.MD.A.3. Apply the area and perimeter formulas for rectangles in real-world and mathematical problems. For example, find the width of a rectangular room given the area of the flooring and the length by viewing the area formula as a multiplication equation with an unknown factor.

Uncovering Student Understanding About the Key Concepts

Using the Naming the Perimeter Probe can provide the following information about how students are thinking about the formula and procedure for finding the perimeter of a rectangle.

Do they

- apply a correct procedure for finding the perimeter of   OR a rectangle?
- correctly account for the length of the two unlabeled   OR sides?

Do they

- confuse perimeter with area or otherwise miscalculate the perimeter?
- omit the unlabeled sides or use incorrect measures for their calculation?

Do they

- show flexible thinking about alternative calculations for finding perimeter?

OR

- write an explanation of their approach that shows an understanding of both perimeter of rectangles and equivalent expressions?

OR

Do they

- fail to recognize equivalent expressions for the perimeter of the rectangle?

- have trouble explaining their approach and answer?

Exploring Excerpts From Educational Resources and Related Research

Common areas of difficulty for students:

[Only 60 percent of fourteen-year-olds could calculate the distance a referee ran around a rugby field when given the length and width of the field.] By the age of 13 years, it is expected that children can find the area of rectangles using a formula, but almost one-third of 13-year-olds use the perimeter formula instead of the area formula when finding a missing dimension. (Ryan & Williams, 2007, p. 101)

Some students interchange perimeter and area, especially if both concepts were initially introduced at almost the same time. (Bay Area Mathematics Task Force, 1999, p. 31)

Differentiating perimeter from area is facilitated by having students draw congruent rectangles and measure, mark off, and label the unit lengths all around the perimeter on one rectangle, then do the same on the other rectangle but also draw the square units. This enables students to see the units involved in length and area and find patterns in finding the lengths and areas of non-square and square rectangles (MP7). (Common Core Standards Writing Team, 2012a, p. 18)

Perimeter problems often give only one length and one width, thus remembering the basic formula can help to prevent the usual error of only adding one length and one width. The formula $P = 2l + 2w$ emphasizes the step of multiplying the total of the given lengths by 2. Students can make a transition from showing all length units along the sides of a rectangle or all area units within (as in Grade 3, p. 18) by drawing a rectangle showing just parts of these as a reminder of which kind of unit is being used. Writing all of the lengths around a rectangle can also be useful. Discussions of formulas such as P = 2*l* + 2*w* can note that unlike area formulas, perimeter formulas combine length measurements to yield a length measurement. (Common Core Standards Writing Team, 2012a, p. 21)

In Grade 4 and beyond, the mental visual images for perimeter and area from Grade 3 can support students in problem solving with these concepts. When engaging in the mathematical practice of reasoning abstractly and quantitatively (MP2) in work with area and perimeter, students think of the situation and perhaps make a drawing. Then they recreate the "formula" with specific numbers and one unknown number as a situation equation for this particular numerical situation. (Common Core Standards Writing Team, 2012a, p. 22)

Surveying the Prompts and Selected Responses in the Probe

The Probe consists of one task and eight selected responses. The prompts and selected responses are designed to elicit understandings and common difficulties as described below.

If a student chooses	It is likely that the student
One or more of the correct answers c, e, f, g	• understands that perimeter is found by finding the distance around the rectangle. • understands a variety of strategies and ways to represent perimeter, including doubling the sum of the length and width, adding all four sides, and doubling each of the sides and taking the sum. • uses an understanding of rectangles to correctly determine the length of each of the unlabeled sides [See Sample Student Response 1]. *Look for indication of the student's understanding in the written explanations of how the student got the answer.*
a	• confuses the area formula with the perimeter formula [See Sample Student Response 2].
b	• fails to include the lengths of the unlabeled sides of the rectangle [See Sample Student Response 3].
d	• applies an incorrect formula that incorporates parts of both the area and perimeter formulas [See Sample Student Response 2].
h	• thinks about the process correctly but ignores the need for grouping symbol [See Sample Student Response 2].

Teaching Implications and Considerations

Ideas for eliciting more information from students about their understanding and difficulties:

- If students have identified some but not all of the correct expressions, ask them, for the ones they missed, to explain how they determined that these expressions did not represent the perimeter.
- If students have selected incorrect expressions, ask questions such as
  - "What does perimeter mean? Can you show me the perimeter of the rectangle?"
  - "What is area? How are area and perimeter different?"
  - "What is the length of the two unlabeled sides? How do you know?"

Ideas for planning instruction in response to what you learned from the results of administering the Probe:

- Provide experiences using concrete materials such as geoboards and making visual representations using centimeter grid paper.
- Give problems in context to help build understanding of perimeter and area—covering a floor with carpet tiles versus installing a fence around a yard.
- Engage students in kinesthetic experiences—walking the perimeter of a large rectangle on the floor and measuring it in paces or tiling a large rectangle with sheets of paper or other materials.

Sample Student Responses to Naming the Perimeter

Responses That Suggest Understanding

Sample Student Response 1

Student chose "e, f, and g" and wrote, "All of these do the same thing. You need to add 2 sevens and 2 fours but that is same as 7 × 2 and 4 × 2. It is also the same to add 4 and 7 first then double. All are correct ways of doing perimeter."

Responses That Suggest Difficulty

Sample Student Response 2

Student chose "a" and "f," and wrote, "This work for rectangles because one is inside and one is outside."

Sample Student Response 3

Student chose "a" and "b," and wrote, "I looked for ones with only a 4 and 7 in it."

Sample Student Response 4

Student chose "d," "e," "f," "g," and "h," and wrote, "You need two 4's and two 7s because there are 4 sides. Two sides with 7 and 2 sides with 4."

Sample Student Response 5

Student chose "e," "f," and "h," and wrote, "These are the different ways to get perimeter. All of them add the four numbers around the outside of the rectangle."

Volume of the Box

Find the volume of each box below.

Circle the correct answer:	Explain your choice:
1. 6 m 3 m 10 m a. 28 m³ b. 180 m³ c. I can't determine the volume	
2. 30 square meters 4 m a. 34 m³ b. 120 m³ c. I can't determine the volume	

Teacher Notes: Volume of the Box

Questions to Consider About the Key Mathematical Concepts

When solving problems involving geometric measurement, can students determine the volume of a rectangular prism? To what extent, do they

- make sense of information given in a three-dimensional figure as it pertains to finding volume?
- demonstrate their understanding of finding volume both conceptually and procedurally?
- describe how different types of information given about rectangular prisms can be used to determine volume?

Common Core Connection (5.MD)

Grade: Fifth

Domain: Measurement and Data

Cluster:

C. Geometric Measurement: Understand concepts of volume.

5.MD.C.5b. Apply the formulas $V = l \times w \times h$ and $V = b \times h$ for rectangular prisms to find volumes of right rectangular prisms with whole-number edge lengths in the context of solving real-world and mathematical problems.

Uncovering Student Understanding About the Key Concepts

Using the Volume of the Box Probe can provide the following information about how the students are thinking about the connections between area and volume measurements.

Do they

- have a conceptual and procedural understanding of area and volume?

OR

- correctly find volume given a variety of types of information?

OR

Do they

- use the volume formula as a basis for a list of steps to follow to find an answer?

- only process information if it is given in a way that fits nicely in the volume formula?

Exploring Excerpts From Educational Resources and Related Research

Common areas of difficulty for students:

If students move rapidly to using formulas without an adequate conceptual foundation in area and volume, many students could have underlying confusions that would interfere with their working meaningfully with measurements. (NCTM, 2000, p. 242)

[There is] a distinction between understanding a formula numerically and understanding it quantitatively. (NCTM, 2003, p. 101)

Students often have preconceived ideas or even misconceptions and may know a list of steps or algorithms. Although they can perform these calculations, they may not always understand the concept or mathematical connections. (Hartweg, 2011, p. 41)

Surveying the Prompts and Selected Responses in the Probe

The Probe consists of two selected response items, each with three choices. The prompts and selected responses are designed to elicit understandings and common difficulties as described below.

If a student chooses	It is likely that the student
1. b 2. b (correct answers)	• understands volume conceptually and reasons about the information given to accurately find the volume of the rectangular prism [See Sample Student Response 1]. *Look for indication of the student's understanding in the written explanations of how the student got the answer.*
2. c	• does not have a conceptual understanding of volume as base × height or doesn't understand that the base doesn't have to be on the bottom of the shape [See Sample Student Response 2].
1. a 2. a	• views the formula as adding the three dimensions of the rectangular prism [See Sample Student Response 3].

Teaching Implications and Considerations

Ideas for eliciting more information from students about their understanding and difficulties:

- What is volume? How do you find the volume of a rectangular prism?
- What dimensions are used to find volume?
- How are area and volume related? How are they different?

Ideas for planning instruction in response to what you learned from the results of administering the Probe:

- Emphasis should be on building understanding of the concepts of area and volume rather than on merely applying formulas.
- Geometric formulas should be learned through exploration and discovery.
- Students should be able to make connections between a formula and an actual object.
- "Students can be at different levels of sophistication concerning length, area, and volume. The assumption that students can and must learn about length concepts first, then area, then volume frequently does not hold true." (NCTM, 1993, p. 79)

Sample Student Responses to Volume of the Box

Responses That Suggest Understanding

Sample Student Response 1

Student chose "b" on Problem 1 and wrote, "The 10 and the 3 and the 6 are the *l* and the *w* and the *h*. Multiply to find volume." Student chose "b" on Problem 2 and wrote, "The 30 could be 6 by 5 or 10 by 3 or any 2 numbers that multiply by 30. The 6 × 5 looks right to me. So 6 × 5 time the other 4 is the volume."

Responses That Suggest Difficulty

Sample Student Response 2

Student chose the correct response "b" on Problem 1 and wrote, "Multiply the 3 numbers." and chose an incorrect response "c" on Problem 2 and wrote, "There are only 2 numbers not 3."

Sample Student Response 3

Student chose "a" for Problem 1 and wrote, "Not sure what to do so I added the numbers." Student chose "a" for Problem 2 and wrote, "Same thing. I added."

Classifying Angles Card Sort

(Reproducible student cards follow Teacher Notes on p. 173.)

Advance Preparation: Create cards by photocopying and cutting out as cards. Separate the three blank cards and the three label cards from the deck and shuffle the rest of the cards.

Instructions:

1. Invite the students to sort the cards into three piles: **Obtuse, Acute,** and **Right**. Use the label cards to identify the piles.

2. As students finish the sort, give them the blank cards and ask them to create their own **Obtuse, Acute,** and **Right** cards.

3. Either choose two cards for the students or ask them to choose two cards from the **Obtuse** pile. Ask the students to explain or show how they knew these cards should go in the **Obtuse** pile.

4. Either choose two cards for the students or ask them to choose two cards from the **Acute** pile. Ask the students to explain or show how they knew these cards should go in the **Acute** pile.

5. Either choose two cards for the students or ask them to choose two cards from the **Right** pile. Ask the students to explain or show how they knew these cards should go in the **Right** pile.

Teacher Notes:
Classifying Angles Card Sort

Questions to Consider About the Key Mathematical Concepts

Do students understand the concept of an angle and how to classify angles as right, obtuse, or acute and describe angles within figures? To what extent do they

- demonstrate an understanding of the definitions of these three types of angles?
- explain their reasoning for how they sort angles and figures?

Common Core Connection (4.G)

Grade: Fourth

Domain: Geometry

Cluster:

A. Draw and identify lines and angles, and classify shapes by properties of their lines and angles.

4.G.A.2. Classify two-dimensional figures based on the presence or absence of parallel or perpendicular lines, or the presence or absence of angles of a specified size. Recognize right triangles as a category, and identify right triangles.

Uncovering Student Understanding About the Key Concepts

Using the Classifying Angles Card Sort Probe can provide the following information about how students are thinking about angle concepts and the terminology to describe angle measures.

Do they

- pay attention to the angle size when determining how to classify an angle?

OR

- apply an understanding of acute, obtuse, and right angles by accurately identifying them in drawings and figures?

OR

- explain the reasoning behind their sorting decisions?

Do they

- pay attention to other attributes such as the length of the rays of the angle or size of the triangle?

- confuse or interchange terminology?

OR

- have difficulty explaining their reasoning?

Exploring Excerpts From Educational Resources and Related Research

Common areas of difficulty for students:

Students often think that angles with longer rays are larger than angles with shorter rays when the angle measurement is exactly the same. Rather than a common method of teaching about angle concepts using visual examples on a blackboard, using large physical spaces and experiences can be more effective in building angle concept and avoiding this length-of-rays misconception. (Munier, Devichi, & Merle, 2008, pp. 402–407)

When people think, they do not always use definitions of concepts, but rather, concept images—a combination of all the mental pictures and properties that have been associated with the concept. Students who not only know a correct verbal description of a concept but also have strongly associated a specific visual image, or concept image, with the concept may have difficulty applying the verbal description correctly. (NCTM, 2003 p. 163)

Surveying the Prompts and Selected Responses in the Probe

The Probe consists of sixteen cards (eight figures, five angles, and three blank cards). The cards have arrows pointing to the angle to be identified. In the set, there are five acute angle cards, four right angle cards, and four obtuse angle cards. Additionally, there are cards with the labels "obtuse," "acute," and "right" for designating the three sort piles. The cards are designed to elicit understandings and common difficulties as described below.

If a student sorts	It is likely that the student
A, C, G, J, M: Acute E, F, K, L: Obtuse B, D, H, I: Right (correct responses)	• understands labels and terminology and can correctly match them to angles. • identifies interior angles within a triangle and can describe the type of angle using appropriate language [See Sample Student Response 1]. *Look for indication of the student's understanding in the written explanations of how the student got the answer.*
A, C, G, J: Obtuse	• confuses acute and obtuse definitions or is paying attention to the exterior reflex angle rather than the interior angle [See Sample Student Response 2].

If a student sorts	It is likely that the student
M: Right Various other choices	• identifies the right angle symbol but misapplies it to another angle within the triangle or figure [See Sample Student Response 3]. • identifies angles that look like right angles as right angles and adds the symbol on the card [See Sample Student Response 4].
J, I: Obtuse F, L: Acute	• interprets acute and obtuse in relation to the length of rays or sides rather than with the measure of angles; relatively smaller drawings are named *acute* and relatively larger drawings are named *obtuse* regardless of angle measures [See Sample Student Response 5].
H, B: Acute or Obtuse	has difficulty interpreting the atypical orientation of an angle or triangle [See Sample Student Response 6].

Teaching Implications and Considerations

Ideas for eliciting more information from students about their understanding and difficulties:

- For students who have sorted correctly but whose explanations are not clear or complete, ask them to explain why they sorted the card as they did. Listen for interpretation of right angle symbol, comparison of the angle to 90 degrees, and use of terminology.
- For students who have sorted a card incorrectly, ask them to explain why they put the card where they did. Also, read their explanations to identify potential sources of difficulty or misunderstanding.

Ideas for planning instruction in response to what you learned from the results of administering the Probe:

- In addition to having students identify angles within shapes, provide opportunities for students to draw angles and figures to build their understanding of the terminology. "[M]athematical terms are useful in communicating geometric ideas, but more important is that constructing examples of these concepts, such as drawing angles and triangles that are acute, obtuse, and right help students form richer concept images connected to verbal definitions." (Common Core Standards Writing Team, 2012b, p. 14)
- "To address misconception that angles with shorter rays are smaller than angles with longer rays, provide opportunities for directly compare these types of angles by placing one over the other. This

activity can help focus on the attribute of spread of the rays rather than the length of the rays." (Van de Walle et al., 2013, p. 395)

- Give students practice with angle measuring tools such as protractors and angle rulers in order to build connections between angle spread, numeric measurement, and angle classification name.

Sample Student Responses to Classifying Angles Card Sort

Responses That Suggest Understanding

Sample Student Response 1

Student categorized all cards correctly and wrote, "I am confident with my card sort because I used the corner of a piece of paper to test the angles. If it fit perfect then it is a right angle. If it is smaller it is acute and if it is bigger it is obtuse."

Responses That Suggest Difficulty

Sample Student Response 2

Student categorized all obtuse as acute and all obtuse as acute and wrote for explanation, "Obtuse means less than 90 and acute means more than 90."

Sample Student Response 3

Student categorized B, D, H, I, and M as right triangles and wrote, "All of these have that symbol on the shape."

Sample Student Response 4

Student categorized B, D, G, H, I, and M as right triangles and wrote, "All of these have that symbol on the shape or I added it to places that are 90 degrees."

Sample Student Response 5

Student categorized I as obtuse and wrote, "The lines on that side are longer so it is obtuse."

Sample Student Response 6

Student categorized B as acute and wrote, "It looks smaller than a corner angle."

What's the Angle? Cards for Sort

6.4A

OBTUSE	ACUTE
RIGHT	

A.

B.

C.

D.

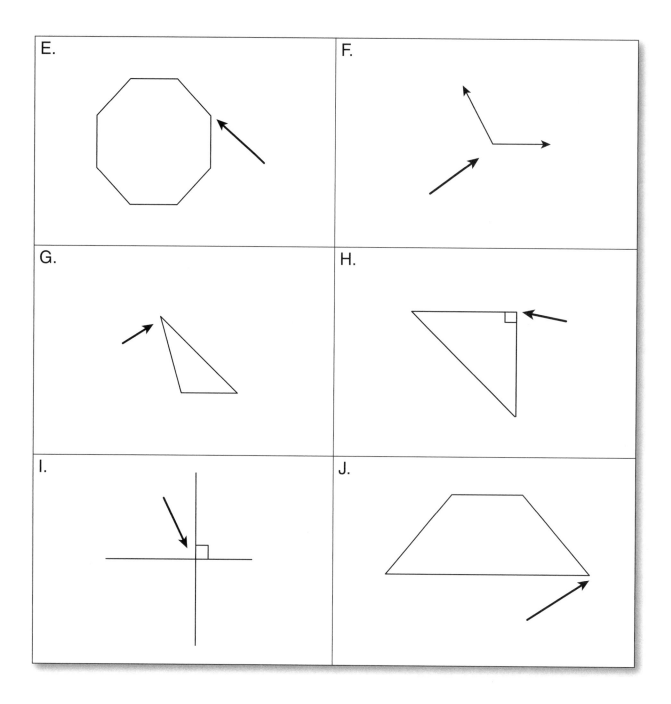

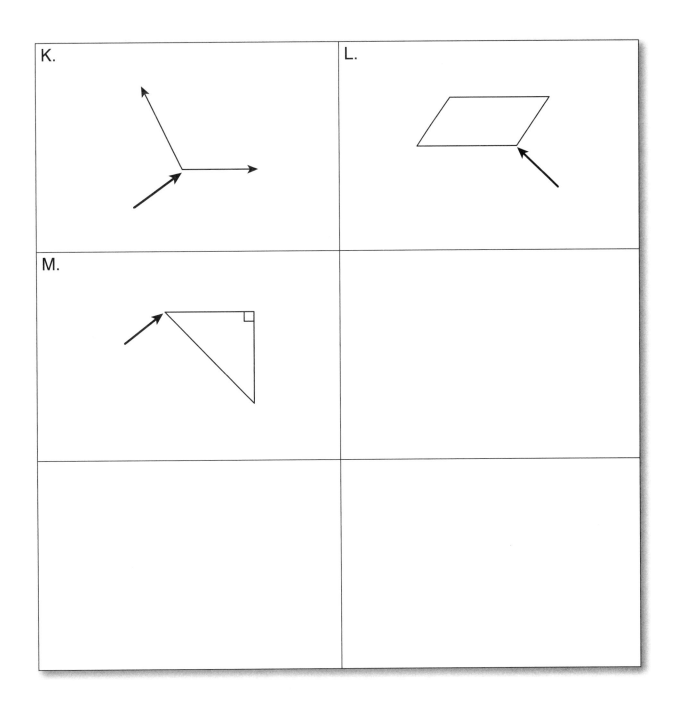

Variation: What's the Angle?

Each figure shows one angle marked by an arrow. Decide if the marked angle is acute, obtuse, or right. Explain your choice.

	What kind of angle is the one marked with the arrow?	Explain:
A.	Acute Obtuse Right	
B.	Acute Obtuse Right	
C.	Acute Obtuse Right	

Each figure shows one angle marked by an arrow. Decide if the marked angle is acute, obtuse, or right. Explain your choice.

	What kind of angle is the one marked with the arrow?	Explain:
D.	Acute Obtuse Right	
E.	Acute Obtuse Right	
F.	Acute Obtuse Right	

Names of the Shape

Circle all correct names for each shape. The side lengths are labeled in units.	Explain your thinking:
1. 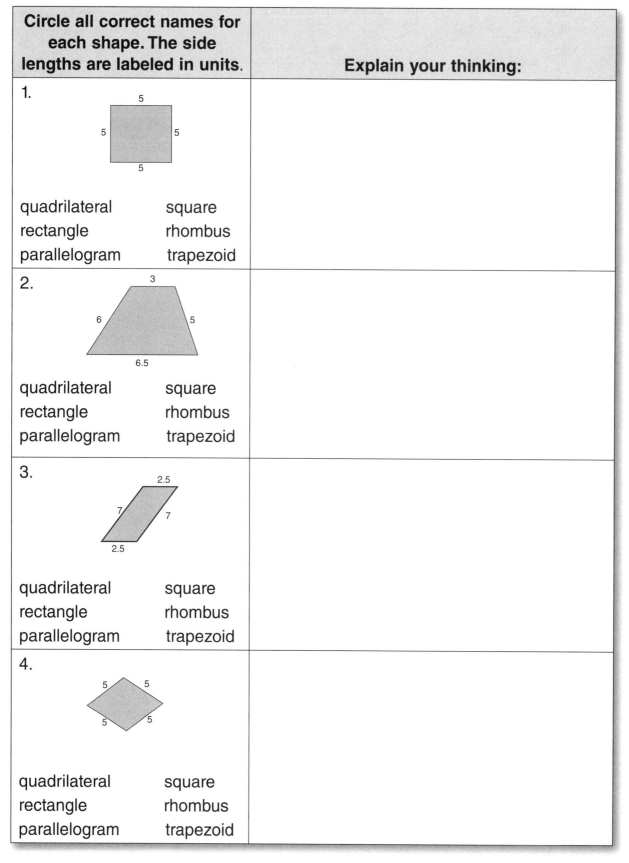 quadrilateral square rectangle rhombus parallelogram trapezoid	
2. quadrilateral square rectangle rhombus parallelogram trapezoid	
3. quadrilateral square rectangle rhombus parallelogram trapezoid	
4. quadrilateral square rectangle rhombus parallelogram trapezoid	

Teacher Notes: Names of the Shape

Questions to Consider About the Key Mathematical Concepts

Do students understand the properties and characteristics of special types of quadrilaterals? To what extent, do they

- distinguish between the relationships and hierarchies between and among subcategories?
- understand that a shape can be placed in more than one category?

Common Core Connection (5.G)

Grade: Fifth

Domain: Geometry

Cluster:

B. Classify two-dimensional figures into categories based on their properties.

5.G.B.3. Understand that attributes belonging to a category of two-dimensional figures also belong to all subcategories of that category. For example, all rectangles have four right angles and squares are rectangles, so all squares have four right angles.

5.G.B.4. Classify two-dimensional figures in a hierarchy based on properties.

Uncovering Student Understanding About the Key Concepts

Using the Names of the Shape Probe can provide the following information about how students are thinking about classifying quadrilaterals.

Do they

- use properties of quadrilaterals to determine which category or categories?

OR

- determine all possible categories?

Do they

- make decisions based on the appearance of the shape?

OR

- think each shape can only belong to one category?

Exploring Excerpts From Educational Resources and Related Research

Common areas of difficulty for students:

No single test exists to pigeonhole students at a certain level [of geometric reasoning]. At the upper elementary grades students should be pushed from level 1 to level 2. If students are not able to follow logical arguments or are not comfortable with conjectures and if-then reasoning, these students are likely still at level 1 or below. (Van de Walle, 2007, p. 414)

One way that children form a concept is to begin with a few cases and by averaging their features develop an "average representation" or prototype, which they use to categorize new examples (Reif, 1987). Children may form prototypes that include extraneous or even erroneous features that can lead to misconceptions, such as thinking of a shape only in terms of cases in standard orientation. (Fuys & Liebov, 2002, p. 156)

Students' responses to initial categorization suggest that their knowledge of the polygons' mathematical properties is largely limited to the number of sides and angles and do not refer to any other mathematical properties. (adapted from Mack, 2007, p. 245)

Surveying the Prompts and Selected Responses in the Probe

The Probe consists of four items, each with the list of categories of quadrilaterals. The prompts and selected responses are designed to elicit understandings and common difficulties as described below.

If a student chooses	It is likely that the student
1. quadrilateral, parallelogram, rectangle, square, rhombus 2. quadrilateral, trapezoid 3. quadrilateral, parallelogram 4. quadrilateral, rhombus (correct responses)	• understands the hierarchies of categories and uses properties of the shape to determine the categories [See Sample Student Response 1]. *Look for indication of the student's understanding in the written explanations of how the student got the answer.*
1. square 2. trapezoid 3. parallelogram 4. rhombus	• thinks the most restrictive category is the correct way to name the shape [See Sample Student Response 2].

If a student chooses	It is likely that the student
1. excludes rhombus or rectangle	• does not realize a square can also be named a rhombus or a rectangle [See Sample Student Response 3].
2. includes parallelogram	• is viewing a parallelogram as a quadrilateral that has at least one pair of parallel sides [See Sample Student Response 4].
3. includes rhombus	• is viewing a rhombus as a quadrilateral that is tilted rather than having four congruent sides [See Sample Student Response 5].

Teaching Implications and Considerations

Ideas for eliciting more information from students about their understanding and difficulties:

- Is it possible to have more than one name for a shape? Why or why not?
- Can you tell me why you circled these names?
- Can you tell me why you didn't include these names?
- Can you create additional examples that show what a [*name a quadrilateral type*] is?

Ideas for planning instruction in response to what you learned from the results of administering the Probe:

- Provide students with materials and structured opportunities to explore shapes and their attributes.
- Students should analyze characteristics and properties of two- and three-dimensional shapes.
- Students should sort quadrilaterals by looking at both examples and nonexamples of special types.
- Students should engage in mathematical conjectures about geometric relationships, such as why a square is a rectangle, but a rectangle is not always a square.
- Students need to develop more-precise ways to describe shapes using mathematics vocabulary associated with trapezoids, parallelograms, rectangles, rhombi, and squares.
- Use interactive technology to have students sort shapes by various attributes.

Sample Student Responses to Names of the Shape

Responses That Suggest Understanding

Sample Student Response 1

Student chose "quadrilateral" and "trapezoid" on Problem 2 and wrote, "I looked at each word and decided whether to circle or cross out. Circled Quad because 4 sides. Circled Trap because 4 sides and 2 are parallel. Not rectangle or square because not 90 degree angles. Not Parall because the slanted sides would connect if make them longer. No Rhom because sides are not same size."

Responses That Suggest Difficulty

Sample Student Response 2

Student chose "square" on Problem 1 and wrote, "Square has 4 sides all the same size and 4 corner angles."

Sample Student Response 3

Student chose "quadrilateral" and "square" on Problem 1 and wrote, "Any 4 sided shape is a quadrilateral and a square has 4 perfect corners and 4 sides as with same length. A rectangle has two sides longer so this isn't one. A rhombus is slanted so this isn't one. A parallelogram is also slanted so this isn't one."

Sample Student Response 4

Student chose "quadrilateral," "parallelogram," and "trapezoid" on Problem 2 and wrote, "Quad means 4 and this shape has 4 sides and angles. Parallelograms have sides that won't cross like the sides that are 3 and 6.5 long. Trapezoids have sides that will cross like the sides that are 6 and 5 long."

Sample Student Response 5

Student chose "rhombus" on Problem 3 and wrote, "Looks like a tilted rectangle."

7

Additional Considerations

An assessment activity can help learning if it provides information that teachers and their students can use as feedback in assessing themselves and one another and in modifying the teaching and learning activities in which they are engaged. (Black, Harrison, Lee, Marshall, & Wiliam, 2004, p. 10)

Mathematics Assessment Probes represent an approach to diagnostic assessment. They can be used for formative assessment purposes if the information about students' understandings and misunderstandings gained from them is used to move students' learning forward. This chapter discusses a variety of considerations for the many applications of Probes, including using them to

- establish learning targets,
- promote individual student reflection,
- conduct student interviews,
- address individual learning needs,
- promote math talk,
- support the Common Core Mathematical Practices, and
- promote professional collaboration and dialogue about math among teachers within and across grade levels.

Since the first Uncovering Student Thinking resource was in development, we have worked with and learned from the many teachers who have implemented our assessment Probes or have developed their own assessment Probes to use with their students. Observing classes, trying out strategies ourselves with students, and listening to teachers describe their experiences and approaches have helped us capture various images from practice over time. Each of the considerations for using Probes is accompanied by a vignette from practice to highlight features of a particular instructional approach.

ESTABLISHING LEARNING TARGETS

> Stating and sharing intended outcomes of learning and assessment is really the foundation for all formative assessment activities. (Wylie et al., 2012, p. 22)

Establishing learning targets and sharing criteria for success in meeting the targets is the foundation of the embedded formative assessment process (CCSSO, 2008; Heritage, 2010; Moss & Brookhart, 2012; Wiliam, 2011; Wylie et al., 2012). The need to develop students' content knowledge, including knowledge of the important mathematics concepts, procedures, and skills outlined in the Common Core Mathematical Standards and Practices, is a priority for mathematics educators. In order for students to meet these established expectations, instruction and assessment must take place with a clear learning target in mind. Standards should inform teachers' thinking about learning targets as an interconnected cluster of learning goals that develop over time. By clarifying the specific ideas and skills described in the standards and articulating them as specific lesson-level learning targets aligned to criteria for success, teachers are in a better position to uncover the gap between students' existing knowledge or skill and the knowledge or skill described in the learning target and criteria for success.

Assessment Probe Use Related to Learning Targets

Each Probe addresses a key mathematical concept related to a Common Core mathematics content standard(s), providing an example of how subsets of mathematics standards can be developed as learning goals. The example in Figure 7.1, from the Fraction Estimates: Addition Probe, highlights three components of the Teacher Notes helpful in determining learning targets: Questions to Consider About the Key Mathematic Concepts, Common Core Connection, and Uncovering Student Understanding About Key Concepts. These features of the Teacher Notes pages can be helpful for developing learning targets that address important conceptual math ideas.

Figure 7.1   Excerpts From Teacher Notes for Fraction Estimates: Addition

Questions to Consider About the Key Mathematical Concepts

When solving problems involving estimation of the addition of two fractions, can students reason about the size of the numbers and the effect of the operation? To what extent do they

- make sense of size of the fractions involved in the problem?
- make sense of the effect of combining the fractions?
- describe how to use this information to determine a reasonable estimation?

Common Core Connection (5.NF)

Grade: Fourth

Domain: Number and Operations—Fractions

Cluster:

B. Build fractions from unit fractions.

4.NF.B.3. Understand a fraction $\frac{a}{b}$ with $a > 1$ as a sum of fractions $\frac{1}{b}$.

4.NF.B.3a. Understand addition and subtraction of fractions as joining and separating parts referring to the same whole.

Uncovering Student Understanding About the Key Concepts

Using the Fraction Estimates: Addition Probe can provide the following information about how students are thinking about the effect of combining fractions.

Do they

- reason correctly about the size of the numbers?   OR
- reason about the size of the product?   OR
- use reasoning to determine whether the sum is greater or less than a given benchmark?   OR

Do they

- apply incorrect benchmarking strategies?
- apply an overgeneralization of "multiplication always results in a bigger answer"?
- use an algorithm to determine an exact answer to compare the given benchmark?

Many teachers we work with are establishing learning targets on a daily basis and are using the Probes as a tool both to support the development of a learning target prior to a lesson and to help students during a lesson reach the learning target.

When using a Probe to support the development of a learning target prior to a lesson, teachers give the Probe to students one to three days prior to the upcoming lesson or unit of instruction. They analyze the evidence gathered from the assessment to gauge students' current understandings and misunderstandings and use this information to develop a learning target or set of learning targets.

The following image from practice provides an example of using a Probe prior to the start of a lesson or set of lessons.

Learning Target: Vignette

In preparation for beginning work with adding fractions, I wanted to get a sense of what my students understood about adding fractions and foundational ideas necessary for understanding fraction addition. In particular, I wondered about how my students conceptualized a fraction both as a part of a whole and as a quantity and what strategies they used to reason about the sums. I also wondered if they thought about the operation of addition as combining. I knew that my students had worked with representing and comparing fractions in previous grades and decided that the Fraction Estimates: Addition Probe (page 122) would be helpful for collecting some information to try to answer my questions. I have discovered that asking students to estimate rather than calculate is a really good way to get at conceptual understanding. Estimating can be more cognitively demanding than applying an algorithm. Sometimes the reason students have difficulty estimating is because they lack conceptual understanding that helps them reason about the size of the fraction and the operation of addition.

My students completed the Probe during our math "Do Now" block of time at the opening of the lesson a few days before I planned to introduce the unit on adding fractions. In reviewing the students' responses to the Probe, I noticed the following:

- A number of my students used the approach of estimating percent equivalents and adding those to determine whether the sum was more or less than the benchmark. They used this strategy effectively and many used this strategy across each of the problems on the Probe.
- A handful of students misapplied whole number thinking such as adding the numerators and adding the denominators to find the sum of the fractions. These students did not use estimation at all.
- Another group of students did not estimate but rather correctly applied the addition algorithm to find the sum of the fractions. While these students got correct answers, their lack of estimation raised questions for me about their ability to reason about the size of the fractions and the operation of addition.
- Only a few students used varied estimation strategies to choose the correct selected response and supported their selection with solid reasoning.

Administering the Probe prior to preparing for a unit helped confirm for me the extent to which students have some foundational understandings. There was evidence that many of my students were not demonstrating that they are able to reason about the size of the fractions. Many, though, did demonstrate some understanding of the operation of addition. This helped me determine a starting point, informing my development of the following learning target and success criteria:

Learning Target: I will understand how reasoning about the size of fractions is helpful in determining estimates for the sum of two fractions.

Success Criteria 1: I can use a strategy to determine whether a sum is larger or smaller then a given benchmark.

Success Criteria 2: I can explain the strategies I use to estimate sums of fractions.

Administering the Probe before beginning the unit of instruction also helped me think about which students might need extra support during initial stages of instruction, and about what content to consider for extension activities for students who already demonstrated some understanding of these foundational concepts.

INDIVIDUAL METACOGNITION AND REFLECTION (THE 4CS)

> The Conceptual Change Model begins with having students become aware of their own thinking. Through a series of developmental steps, it helps them to confront their views and to refine them if necessary, then to immediately use their new understanding. (Stepans, Schmidt, Welsh, Reins, & Saigo, 2005, p. 37)

The conceptual change model as described by Stepans and colleagues (2005) takes into consideration recommendations from research and is rooted in the learning cycle approach. The goal of the conceptual change model is to uncover students' current ideas about a topic before teaching new content related to the topic. Students learn by integrating new knowledge with what they already know and can do. Sometimes this new knowledge is integrated in a way that contributes to or builds on an existing misunderstanding. However, if ideas are elicited prior to instruction, existing preconceptions and/or misconceptions can be confronted explicitly, minimizing situations in which students are trying to integrate new knowledge into a flawed or underdeveloped framework of ideas. This explicit confrontation of preconceptions or misconceptions creates cognitive dissonance in which students begin to question and rethink their preconceptions, and further instruction and reflection can now help students understand the new concept. Our 4Cs Model, an adaptation of the conceptual change model, consists of four stages, as shown in Figure 7.2.

Figure 7.2 The 4Cs Model

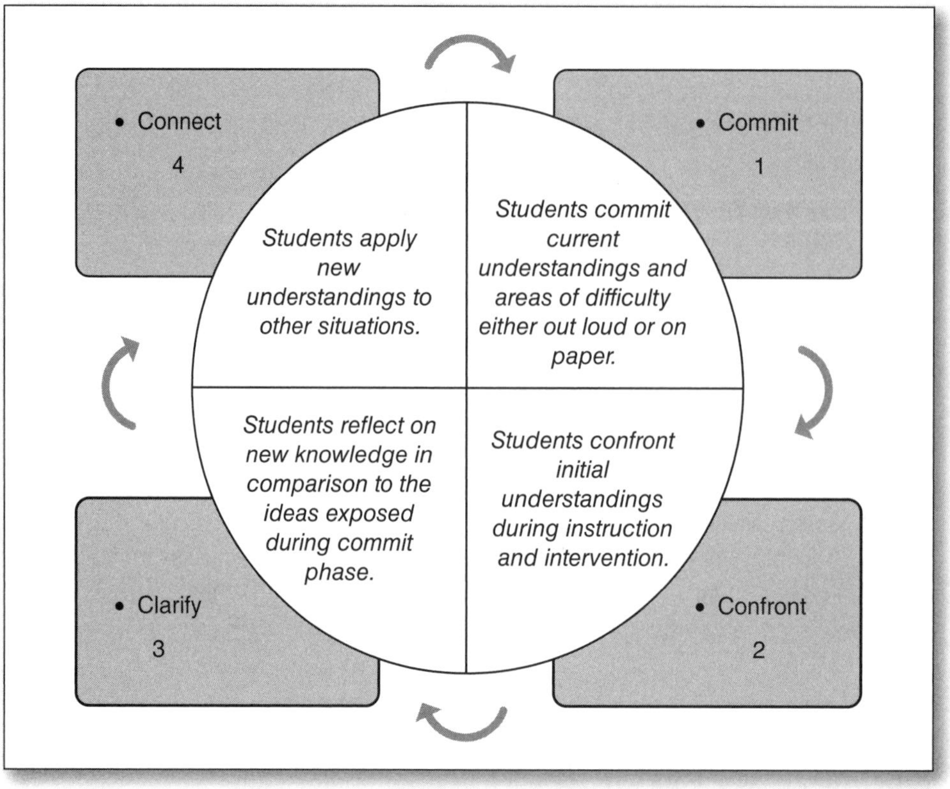

Source: Tobey & Fagan (2013).

At this point, you may be wondering how the 4Cs model connects with the QUEST Cycle that is central to the use of the Probes in this book. The QUEST Cycle is written from a teacher's point of view and implicitly incorporates the 4Cs model. Since even the most effective teachers cannot do the actual learning for their students, the 4Cs model provides the critical student perspective.

Assessment Probe Use Related to the 4Cs Model

Teachers using the 4Cs Model in conjunction with assessment Probes typically use the following process:

1. *Commit.* Choose a Probe to elicit ideas related to a learning target. Give the Probe to all students, capturing student responses either by asking them to write explanations, scripting their explanations, or a combination of both.

2. *Confront.* Provide instruction based on results, integrating a variety of anonymous student responses, both correct and incorrect, into the lesson at appropriate junctures and lead class discussion about the responses.

3. *Clarify.* Return students' initial responses to the Probe to them (or read them to students) and ask students to clarify or revise anything in the response based on what they just learned in the lesson.

4. *Connect.* Pose additional questions similar to those in the Probe to assess whether students have met the learning target.

The following image from practice highlights the use of the 4Cs Model.

Sticky Notes Bar Graphs—4Cs in Action: Vignette

As an introduction to a lesson about comparing and naming fractions using the number line, I decided to give my whole class the problem from the Locating a Fraction on a Number Line Probe (page 98). I created a large poster with the number line image and the three students' opinions along the bottom of the poster. I gave each student a sticky note, and asked them to put their initials on the sticky side of the note. (This way, when they posted their opinion, it would remain anonymous to the other students.) Next, I asked them to think individually about this problem and decide who they agreed with. After everyone had some think time, I asked them to place their sticky note on the poster to create a sticky note bar graph according to who they agreed with. (The students' sticky note bar graph is shown in Figure 7.3.) In creating this bar graph, I asked students to commit to an answer and in doing so I learned that there was disagreement about who was correctly naming the fraction shown on the number line.

I expected that at this stage of the unit my students would be in different places in their understanding, and this commit activity confirmed this to be the case. While this information gave me a general idea, it didn't give me information about my students' reasoning. I planned to learn more about their thinking through the next part of the lesson.

In the next part of the lesson, we gathered on our Math Talk carpet to share ideas about how to compare fractions using the number line representation and how to interpret the value of a point on the number line when it is located between two hash marks on a number line. My purpose in this part of the lesson was to elicit more information about student thinking and areas of difficulty. On the easel, I showed the students a number line with

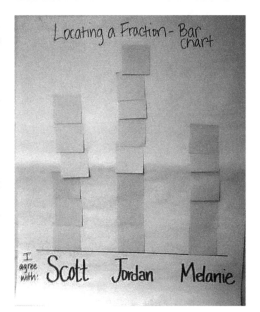

Figure 7.3 Sticky Bar Chart

(Continued)

(Continued)

two points, A and B, and asked them which point represented a larger number. As students discussed their thinking, they talked about the proximity of the points to the labeled hash marks. One student said that a number to the right is always going to be bigger, and we talked about why she thinks this and whether this will always be true. Next, I asked them to turn and talk with a partner about how to name these two points. They had a handout with the number line on it, and I gave them a few minutes to discuss their thinking with their partner. Then, I asked a pair to share what they had discussed. Other pairs built on the thinking and after some discussion, the following exchange occurred:

Student 1: We decided that point A was easier to name because it's not in between the lines. So, we started with that one. The number line has endpoints of 0 and 1 and is broken up into five spaces. Point A is 3 marks over from 0, so it's called $\frac{3}{5}$.

Teacher: Okay, others have also said that this point is $\frac{3}{5}$. Did anyone name this point something else?

Student 2: We called it $\frac{7}{10}$ because we made more lines on the number line to make it into tenths. Then we saw that it was seven over so we called it $\frac{7}{10}$.

Teacher: Can you come up and show us what you did? I'm understanding, I think, that you further partitioned the number line by breaking each of these one-fifths into two parts. After you did that, how big was one of these intervals?

Student 2: One tenth.

Teacher: Okay, why a tenth?

Student 2: Because half of a fifth is a tenth.

Teacher: How did you get $\frac{7}{10}$?

Discussion continued as the student explained the counting they did to get to $\frac{7}{10}$ (included the first hash mark in their count) and others helped to explain that Point A is actually $\frac{6}{10}$.

Teacher: Okay, so now we have two names for Point A: $\frac{6}{10}$ and $\frac{3}{5}$. Did anyone name this point something else?

Student 3: Oh, wait a minute. This is kind of like what we were doing over there (he gestures back to the sticky note bar chart from the beginning of the class). I get it now. I want to change my answer. Can I go move my sticky note?

Teacher: Oh, something that we just talked about is making you rethink your answer to the problem from the beginning of the class. I'm really glad you are making connections between these two problems. Let's finish up what we are working on here. When we finish, I'll help you find your sticky note and you can move it.

The above vignette illustrates the 4Cs in action. Through the sharing of ideas and elaboration in this discussion, this student was able to confront a flawed idea about naming points on the number line, In future parts of the lesson, the student will have more opportunities to connect his new thinking to other problems.

GIVING STUDENT INTERVIEWS

> Whenever we try to get at a student's thinking, we should try to focus not only on what the student is thinking but also on what the student understands about his or her own knowledge. The questions we ask when interviewing a student will help the student become more aware of her own cognitive processes. (Ashlock, 2006, p. 27)

Conducting individual or small group interviews provides information beyond what written student work can provide. Interviewing students offers insight into their level of understanding and their ability to put mathematical ideas into words and/or representations. The interview process also allows teachers to gather information about the range of learning needs within a group of students and is particularly powerful for students whose written expressive language is not reflective of the depth of their understanding. Teachers who regularly incorporate student interviews either selectively interview a subset of students or all of their students, depending on how they wish to use the results.

Assessment Probe Use Related to Student Interviews

Teachers have found that any Probe can be administered as an interview and see benefits to this mode of administration with students at all grade levels. Sometimes the experience of being able to verbalize thinking first can help students build skills to bridge to expressing their thinking in writing. Because the Probes are short, most are manageable to administer as interviews, especially when teachers are selective and strategic about whom to interview.

Many teachers manage individual interviews by conducting them while their students not being interviewed are engaged in other activities. Teachers who utilize stations or have independent reading or math blocks sometimes take these opportunities to interview students. In addition to or in place of individual interviews, teachers also use structured small group interviews during station time. This method allows for individual Level 1 selected responses but, depending on writing capabilities, may rely on a small group discussion for the explanations. When managed well, these conversations provide valuable information about both students' thinking and their ability to build on the ideas of other students to advance their thinking.

One challenge of the small group interview approach is the temptation to jump from information gathering into instruction. Stay focused on and be explicit with students that the goal of this small group activity is for you to listen to their ideas and to ask questions. By doing so, you will get the information you need for planning for upcoming lessons. Informing students of the goal of the interview can also help to avoid confusion for students who may also participate in small intervention groups or other small group work focused on instruction.

The following vignette illustrates the use of two related Probes and interviews in order to address the needs of a small group with related difficulties.

Interviewing Strategies—Student Interviews: Vignette

I administered the Rounding Decimals Probe (page 80) to my whole class and noticed some patterns in responses. In particular there was a small group of students who seemed to have substantial difficulty with naming decimal place values. The work of these students suggested difficulty naming the decimal place values to the right of the decimal point. For example, one student was naming the decimal place values in reverse order and a few of them called the hundredths place the tenths place. I wanted to learn more about their thinking, so I conducted informal interviews with these four students using the Rounding Whole Numbers Probe (page 62), which is a whole number version of the Rounding Decimals Probe (page 80). Since some of these students also receive math support in the learning center, I would use this additional class time for conducting these interviews and putting interventions into place to help address some missing foundational concepts. Administering these two related Probes helped me learn that some students actually had some understanding of rounding whole numbers, but their place values difficulties prevented them from being successful rounding decimals. Gathering this information allowed me to target next steps on the meaning of decimals rather than focusing immediately on rounding.

ADDRESSING INDIVIDUAL NEEDS

Although many teachers feel they lack the time or tools to pre-assess on a regular basis, the data derived from pre-assessment are essential in driving differentiated instruction. (Small, 2009, p. 5)

In addition to using Probes as pre-assessment, understanding how the math content contained in the Probe connects to a progression of math learning can support efforts to differentiate instruction to meet students' needs.

The Common Core State Standards in mathematics (CCSSM) were built on progressions: narrative documents describing the progression of a topic across a number of grade levels, informed both by research on children's cognitive development and by the logical structure of mathematics. These documents were spliced together and then sliced into grade level standards. From that point on the work focused on refining and revising the grade level standards. The early drafts of the progressions documents no longer correspond to the current state of the standards.

It is important to produce up-to-date versions of the progressions documents. They can explain why standards are sequenced the way they are, point out cognitive difficulties and pedagogical solutions, and give more detail on particularly knotty areas of the mathematics. (Institute for Mathematics and Education [IME], University of Arizona, 2007)

Being aware of and understanding a progression of learning of a topic is important when considering how to address the needs of students. Often individual students can be grouped with others who have a similar misunderstanding or who have a similar missing foundational concept that is posing a barrier to learning the mathematics of the learning target. "Compiling an inventory for a set of papers can provide a sense of the class's progress and thus inform decisions about how to differentiate instruction" (Burns, 2005, p. 29). Decisions about next steps should be informed based on the goal of moving students' understanding toward a defined learning target; when the gap between existing knowledge and the learning target is too great, however, students may need to access the content at a "lower" point in the learning progression. This may require developing alternative and additional learning targets, allowing students to build the prerequisite understanding necessary. Probes provide critical information to inform these decisions and are therefore a useful tool for all teachers of math, including special educators, Title I teachers, and interventionists.

The vignette below provides an example of how a teacher uses the card sort Probes.

Card Sort Probes—Is It Equivalent?: Vignette

Card sorts are one of my favorite types of Probes. I find they are engaging for all students and particularly helpful for students who struggle to write their ideas on paper and pencil. I recently had my students complete the Equivalent Fractions Card Sort Probe (page 102) as an individual activity before we began a unit of study on fractions. I made observations during the sort. I sometimes asked students to explain to me how they sorted. I also asked students to use a blank card to write one pair of equivalent fractions.

I use an envelope system that allows me to keep track of each student's sorted cards. At the beginning of the school year, I give each student a small

---

(Continued)

(Continued)

6 × 9 manila envelope along with small letter envelopes labeled "yes" and "no." Students write their names on the manila envelopes and decorate them (see Figure 7.4). When we do a card sort, they place their cards in the small envelopes and put those in the manila envelope.

This system works great for me. If I am not able to make it around to all my students during the sort, I can review their cards later. Having the sets of sorted cards enables me to follow up with students, share information with special education teachers, plan learning targets and create pairings for subsequent lessons.

Figure 7.4 Envelopes for Card Sort Probes

PROMOTING MATH TALK

Because discussions help students to summarize and synthesize the mathematics they are learning, the use of student thinking is a critical element of mathematical discourse. When teachers help students build on their thinking through talk, misconceptions are made clearer to both teacher and student, and at the same time, conceptual and procedural knowledge deepens. (Garcia, 2012, p. 3)

Talking the talk is an important part of learning. (Black & Harrison, 2004, p. 4)

When students are talking about their mathematical ideas—whether in a whole-class discussion, in small groups, or in pairs—they are using the language and conventions of mathematics.

Children learn vocabulary primarily indirectly through their conversations with others and from the books and programs they are exposed to. However, because many words used in mathematics may not come up in everyday contexts—and if they do, they may mean something totally different—math vocabulary needs to be explicitly taught (Minton, 2007). Students' use of math terms is directly related to their experiences. Lack of exposure to math situations and opportunities to develop a correct mathematical vocabulary can deprive students of the language of math. The language of math is specific and uses words to denote not only meaning, but also symbolic notation. Symbols enable mathematical ideas to be expressed in precise ways that reflect quantitative relationships. Misunderstandings about the meaning of a math symbol or notation or how to use it can impact understanding. Just as some words can take on different meanings in different contexts, so can some mathematical symbols.

Assessment Probe Use Related to Promoting Math Talk

In Chapter 1, we used an image from practice to illustrate how assessment Probes can create a link between assessment, instruction, and learning. We remind you of that image here:

In an intermediate classroom, the teacher uses a Probe to uncover students' explanations of how to determine equivalent and nonequivalent products and quotients of various two-digit numbers (for example, is 16 × 24 equal to 24 × 16? Is 36 ÷ 12 equal to 12 ÷ 36)? By creating a bar graph of students' responses to anonymously display students' ideas, the teacher and the class can see that many students believe that both products and quotients are equivalent regardless of the order of the numbers. Knowing that this is a common misunderstanding cited in the research literature and seeing that the data from her own class mirror that misunderstanding, the teacher designs a lesson that involves the students in using visual models to model the multiplication and division of various two-digit numbers. After students experience modeling the operations, they revisit their original ideas and have an opportunity to revise them. The next day, students are given the task of defining the commutative property of multiplication. They work in small groups to demonstrate the property and explain why there is no commutative property for division. At the end of the lesson, students are asked to reflect on their original thinking on the Probe about whether the products and quotients were or were not equivalent. (Adapted from Keeley & Rose Tobey, 2011, p. 2)

The image illustrates how a teacher engages students in discussion using the examples and nonexamples to tease out properties of multiplication and division. The book from which this excerpt is taken, *Mathematics Formative Assessment: 75 Practical Strategies for Linking Assessment, Instruction and Learning,* provides descriptions of specific strategies that can be combined with assessment Probes in order to promote learning through mathematical discourse (Keeley & Rose Tobey, 2011). Many of these strategies have been used or modified for use by teachers in Grades 3–5. Two such strategies, Agreement Circles and the more commonly used Think-Pair-Share, provide a whole group strategy example and a pair/small group example of promoting learning through discourse.

Agreement Circles

Agreement Circles provide a kinesthetic way to activate thinking and engage students in discussing and defending their mathematical ideas. Students stand in a large circle as the teacher reads a statement. The students who agree with the statement step to the center of the circle. Those who disagree remain standing on the outside of the circle. Those in the inner circle face their peers still standing around the outside circle and then divide themselves into small groups of students who agree and disagree. The small groups then engage in discussion to defend their thinking. This is repeated with several rounds of statements relating to the same topic, each time with students starting by standing around the large circle. At the beginning, this strategy works best with Probes that generated substantial disagreement. Over time, once the classroom environment allows for students to take risks and feel safe doing so, the strategy can be successfully used when a smaller range of students choose certain selected responses. (Keeley & Rose Tobey, 2011, pp. 54–55)

Think-Pair-Share

Think-Pair-Share begins by providing students with an opportunity to activate their own thinking. The pairing strategy allows students to first share their ideas with one other person and modify their ideas or construct new knowledge as they interact with their partner. Next, students are asked to share ideas with a larger group. After having had a chance to discuss their ideas with another student as a pair, many students are more comfortable and willing to respond to the whole-group discussion. As a result, the quality of their responses often improves and contributes to an improvement in the quality of the whole group discussion as well. Thoughtful pairing of students helps to ensure that the pair conversation is productive. Consider pairing students with others with whom they will engage productively and whose content level understanding is similar enough for common ground yet reflects differences that will evoke conversation.

In the Think-Square-Share variation, students discuss in groups of four rather than in pairs. When using a Probe with selected response choices, teachers can prearrange groups so that each includes students who chose different selections. In their "square," they have a chance to discuss their thinking and try to justify their reasoning or modify it based on information they gain from the discussion (Keeley & Rose Tobey, 2011, pp. 189–190).

SUPPORTING THE MATHEMATICAL PRACTICES

Formative assessment begins by identifying a learning goal, based on a grade-level standard from the Common Core State Standards (CCSS). The Common Core State Standards for Mathematics (CCSSM) define what students should understand and be able to do in K-12 mathematics. Since the grade-level standards in the CCSSM "define what students should understand and be able to do," it is important for teachers to find out what students know and can do both conceptually and procedurally in relation to the expectation for learning. In addition to these content standards, an important feature of the CCSSM is the Standards for Mathematical Practices. These practices describe a variety of processes and proficiencies that teachers at all grade levels should seek to develop in their students. Since the CCSSM do not define the methods and strategies used to determine the readiness and prior knowledge necessary to achieve the standards, the Mathematics Assessment Probes in this book complement CCSSM's eight Standards for Mathematical Practices and their link to mathematical content (Keeley & Rose Tobey, 2011, p. 30).

Assessment Probe Use Related to the "Reasoning and Explaining" Practice Cluster

Simply using the Mathematics Assessment Probes with students will not result in students who are proficient within this cluster of practices. Instead, use of the Probes over time, combined with higher expectations for reasons and justification for selecting a response, will support students as they progress toward proficiency. Use of the follow-up questions accompanying the Probes (see Figure 7.5 for an example) can help students who are having difficulty describing their reasoning or who give only brief explanations such as "I just knew" or "my teacher told me that."

Figure 7.5 Are They Equivalent? Follow-Up Questions

*T*eaching Implications and Considerations

Ideas for eliciting more information from students about their understanding and difficulties:

- For students who have answered the prompts correctly but whose explanations are not clear or complete, ask them to explain how they determined whether expressions were or were not equivalent. Listen for understanding of place value and reasoning about the operation of multiplication.
- To learn more about students' thinking, ask questions such as

  o "How did you decide on your responses?"
  o "What does it mean for two expressions to be equivalent?"
  o "Can you think of another expression that is equivalent to this one?"

Since students naturally generalize from examples and nonexamples, many of the assessment Probes are structured or can be structured as card sorts, which capitalize on examples and nonexamples of categorizing information to help students build important reasoning skills. Intermediate students are very able to use a variety of ways to justify their answers, including perception, evidence gathered from observation, and reasoning grounded in previously accepted facts or properties. The extent to which students are able to use these skills when giving explanations can be elicited through use of the Probes.

Discussion Group Question Tents—Improving Student Communication: Vignette

I administered the variation Probe Prime or Composite. After students worked individually on the Probe, I put them in groups of three and four to discuss their work. I found these short exchanges invaluable for learning about individual students' reasoning and explanation capabilities. I used the questions provided in the Teacher Notes as a guide to develop a short list of prompts. I made a little question tent for each group (see Figure 7.6). They were able to refer to these questions as they discussed their thinking and listened to others in their group.

Figure 7.6 Prime/Composite Question Tent

- How do you know if a number is **prime** or **composite**?

- Is there a number that you feel confident about? Share your thinking.

- Is there a number you are not sure about? What makes this one difficult for you?

- How do you determine the factors of a number?

Many of the assessment Probes make use of the "math-talk" structure, in which students are asked to decide who they agree with and provide a reason for their choice. (See Locating a Fraction on a Number Line Probe on page 98 for an example of a math-talk Probe.) Probes that are structured in this way provide opportunities for students to critique the reasonableness of another's thinking and justify their findings. Again, using Probes structured in this way only on occasion during the school year will not build students' ability in a meaningful way. Instead, students will need multiple opportunities over the course of the school year and across all of the mathematics domains in order to build these abilities.

In order to become critical thinkers, students need opportunities to explain and justify their own thinking and examine and critique the thinking of others. The math talk Probes offer a great way to provide these experiences in an engaging and depersonalized way. Using these Probes gives students a chance to learn and practice how to interpret and respond to the thinking of others.

When given a math-talk Probe, students first reason about the problem and then compare their thinking and approach to those of several fictitious students.

If they agree with one of the fictitious student's responses, they then need to be able to explain *why* they agree.

The "do, compare, choose, and explain" structure of a math-talk Probe (p. 98) allows time for each student to process and reflect before sharing his or her thinking. In addition, this independent time allows me to observe students' choices as they work and learn about who may be struggling for a particular reason and what patterns are emerging across all of the student responses.

I also use the math-talk Probe structure to design my own math-talk tasks drawing on actual responses that my own students have given. I find that when used strategically these tasks help to confront common difficulties and misconceptions as well as to highlight good mathematical reasoning and explanation.

When students derive answers to problems, we not only need to get at their thinking in order to understand how they obtained those answers, we also need to learn how they justify their answers—how they prove they are correct in their own thinking. We can look for three kinds of justification schemes identified by Sowder and Harel and illustrated by Flores:

- *Externally based schemes* in which a textbook or authority figure is cited as justification.
- *Empirically based schemes* in which students use perception or concrete objects to show that their answer is correct.
- *Analysis use schemes* in which students use counting strategies or state mathematical relations to justify their answers.

As a student's thinking develops over time, we expect to see fewer uses of justification schemes that are externally based. We even hope to see use of empirically based schemes eventually give way to schemes that use analysis, for such thinking is distinctly mathematical. (Ashlock, 2006, p. 28)

In summary, students in Grades 3–5 should be encouraged to make conjectures, be given time to search for evidence to prove or disprove them, and be expected to explain and justify their ideas. Students should be introduced to and be expected to use basic logic words in their explanation, including *not, and, or, all, some, if . . . then,* and *because,* and to incorporate mathematical properties and relationships, rather than authority (e.g., "because my teacher told us"), as the basis for the argument.

Assessment Probe Use Related to the Seeing Structure and Generalizing Practice Cluster

Many of the mathematics targets of the assessment Probes align to the CCSSM content standards directly associated with the Seeing Structure and Generalizing Practice Structure. For example, the Are They Equivalent? Probe (see Figure 7.7) elicits from students whether they understand the commutative property as well as other place value ideas that allow one to check equivalence without actually calculating and comparing the results.

Figure 7.7 Are They Equivalent? Probe

Are They Equivalent?

Without actually calculating, use what you know about multiplying two-digit numbers to decide which of the number expressions below are equivalent to

24 × 16

	Circle one:	Explain your answer:
A. **16 × 24**	Yes No	
B. **26 × 14**	Yes No	
C. **(20 + 4) × 16**	Yes No	
D. **12 × 32**	Yes No	
E. **42 × 61**	Yes No	

Students who are able to choose the correct responses without calculating are likely to be seeing the structure within each of the problem sets. The explanation is key to determining whether, in fact, students are seeing the structure and are able to explain/articulate the reasons for their correct responses.

Assessment Probe Use Related to the Modeling and Using Tools Practice Cluster

Many of the mathematical targets of the assessment Probes align to the Common Core content standards directly associated with the Modeling and Using Tools Practice Cluster. For example, the Comparing Lengths Probe (Figure 7.8) makes use of rulers to determine how the length of a marker compares to that of a pencil.

Figure 7.8   Comparing Lengths Probe

Comparing Lengths

About how much longer is the marker than the pencil?	Choose one:	Explain your answer:
1.	a. $\frac{1}{4}$ unit b. $\frac{1}{2}$ unit c. $\frac{3}{4}$ unit d. 1 unit	
2.	a. They are the same length. b. $\frac{1}{4}$ unit c. 1 unit d. $1\frac{1}{4}$ unit	
3.	a. $\frac{1}{4}$ unit b. $\frac{1}{2}$ unit c. 1 unit d. $1\frac{1}{4}$ unit	

How students make use of the ruler as a tool depends on the foundational conceptual ideas they understand and are able to apply to the Probe context. Once again, it is the explanation prompt that requires students to describe their process and allows the teacher to get a better sense of the students' approach and use of tools.

The area of measurement is one in which our students consistently score relatively lower than in other domains. In part, I think it's because they do not have enough experiences with actual measurement, using measurement tools and developing an understanding of units of measurement.

When I first saw this Probe, I thought it would be a great way to assess my students' understanding of linear measurement; the ruler as a tool; and units and subunits of measurement and comparison. I was eager to try the Probe with my students but I decided to wait to give the Probe until after we had explored some initial measurement activities.

As students were making measurements, I paid attention to common difficulties that would be assessed by the Probe such as different starting points, visual interpretation, and fractional units. I tried to bring out these issues during whole class discussion when possible and even set up some scenarios that would replicate a similar situation.

This Probe gave students an opportunity to demonstrate their ability to abstract from the kinds of concrete physical measurement activities to interpreting visual representations of objects. This kind of abstraction will be important when they move to solving algebraic geometric problems in later years.

The Multiplication and Division Sentences (Number Models) Probe (see Figure 7.9) is an example of a Probe that elicits information about whether students are able to model with mathematics.

Students who can make sense of a story context can determine how to model the situation mathematically using numbers and symbols. They are able to describe how their model relates back to the context and use the model to solve the problem.

In addition to Probes that are directly connected to content standards related to modeling and/or the use of tools, all the assessment Probes have the ability to elicit information regarding this Practice Cluster. For many of the assessment Probes, there is not an expectation that a particular model or tool be used. At the diagnostic stage, more information is gathered about your students if you naturally allow students to request tools to use in determining their response and/or explaining their thinking. For example, when completing the Representing Decimals Probe (p. 110), students may or may not ask for concrete materials to model the problem. When students struggle with this task yet do not ask for materials, they may not yet have the skills to be proficient with this particular practice. An important consideration when using assessment Probes is to combine the use of Probes that expect specific modeling processes or given tools with Probes that expect more varied and open-ended approaches. In this way, you can provide opportunities for students to practice identifying and utilizing helpful tools, and you can learn how their abilities in this area are progressing.

Figure 7.9   Multiplication and Division Sentences (Number Models) Probe

Multiplication and Division Sentences (Number Models)

1. **Alex went for a walk and saw 4 nests each with 3 eggs.**

What number sentence can be used to find the total number of eggs?

Circle one: Explain why you chose that number sentence:

A. $4 + 3 = ?$

B. $4 + 4 + 4 + 4 = ?$

C. $4 \times 3 = ?$

D. $3 \times 3 \times 3 \times 3 = ?$

2. **Min is making gift bags for her friends. If she puts 3 pencils in each bag and she has 12 pencils in all, how many gift bags can she make?**

What number sentence can be used to find the number of gift bags?

Circle one: Explain why you chose that number sentence:

A. $12 \times 3 = ?$

B. $12 + 3 = ?$

C. $12 \div 3 = ?$

D. $3 \div 12 = ?$

Assessment Probe Use Related to the Overarching Habits of Mind of Productive Thinkers Practice Cluster

The assessment Probes can support student metacognition by inviting students to identify the extent of their own understanding of a problem and its solution and to examine and make sense of the problem-solving approaches of others. The Probes relate to this overarching cluster of practices both in terms of the content of the Probes and the ways in which they are used in questioning, instruction, and discussion.

Chapter 1 discusses many of these instructional considerations for using Probes as a bridge between assessment, instruction, and learning.

Many of the Probes require precision in the explanation that supports a selected response (Level 1). For example, in the Are They Equivalent? Probe variation (p. 78), students determine whether expressions are equivalent to 24 × 16. Students who are able to correctly determine yes or no by articulating ideas related to math properties are attending to the precision necessary to solve the problem.

The ideas within the Mathematical Practices must be developed over time and throughout a student's K–12 school experience. During the elementary grades, students can build an important foundation in which they begin to view mathematics as "more than completing sets of exercises or mimicking processes the teacher explains. Doing mathematics means generating strategies for solving problems, applying those approaches, seeing if they lead to solutions, and checking to see whether your answers make sense" (Van de Walle et al., 2013, p. 13). When students view mathematics as interpreting, organizing, inquiring about, and constructing meaning, it becomes creative and alive (Fosnot & Dolk, 2001, p. 13).

SHARING EXPERIENCES AND PROMOTING PROFESSIONAL COLLABORATION

The engine of improvement, growth, and renewal in a professional learning community is collective inquiry. The people in such a school are relentless in questioning the status quo, seeking new methods, testing those methods, and then reflecting on the results. (DuFour, DuFour, Eaker, & Many, 2006, p. 68)

Using Probes provides an opportunity for collaboration among educators as they examine and discuss student work together:

The most important aspect of this strategy is that teachers have access to, and then develop for themselves the ability to understand, the content students are struggling with and ways that they, the teachers, can help. Pedagogical content knowledge—that special province of excellent teachers—is absolutely necessary for teachers to maximize their learning as they examine and discuss what students demonstrate they know and do not know. (Loucks-Horsley, Love, Stiles, Mundry, & Hewson, 2003, p. 183)

By providing research excerpts and instructional implications specific to the ideas of the Probe, the Teacher Notes can guide educators through the action research QUEST Cycle, providing a collaborative framework for examining student thinking together and developing plans for improving instruction.

> Our school is working on an initiative to use formative assessment Probes as part of a cycle of planning instruction. We use Probes to gather initial information about student understanding relative to learning targets and criteria for success and then plan instruction based on what we learn. After a unit of instruction, we readminister a Probe to see how student understanding has progressed. Sometimes, we give students back their original Probe and invite them to make revisions to their work based on what they have learned since they first completed the Probe. We are especially interested in the ways that this approach can help students who are struggling in math. We are fortunate to have regular grade-level common planning meetings. At each meeting we choose a Probe that we will each administer to our students before our next meeting. We each bring a few samples of student work to the next meeting and discuss what we find interesting in our samples and look for patterns and commonalities in strengths and difficulties in the student work. Based on our discussion, we plan strategies that build on the strengths in order to address the difficulties. We then try these strategies/activities with students before the next meeting where we share and reflect on our experiences. The Probes have provided us a really clear way to focus on formative assessment. Since the Probes are related to the common core and research-based misconceptions and are very manageable to administer, they are a great jumping-off point for our common planning.

The above instructional considerations provide information about how to use the Probes as a link between assessment, instruction, and learning. Embedded within each of the images from practice are several ideas for administering the Probes, including the following:

- Card Sort Probes—Is It Equivalent?: Vignette, p. 193
- Sticky Notes Bar Graphs—4Cs in Action: Vignette, p. 189
- Discussion Group Question Tents—Improving Student Communication: Vignette, p. 198
- Interviewing Strategies—Student Interviews: Vignette, p. 192

SUMMARY

An important takeaway about using the Probes is the importance of your role in selecting and scaffolding Probes for use in the classroom. When selecting Probes consider

- how well the content of the Probe aligns to the targeted concepts you want students to learn;

- how well the structure of the Probe lends itself to the mathematical practice you wish students to incorporate; and
- how the Probe will serve as the link between assessment, instruction, and learning.

The first of the considerations, targeting the appropriate math content, was discussed in Chapter 1, where we outlined conceptual and procedural understanding and highlighted where in the Teacher Notes to find information about concepts targeted through a Probe. The second consideration, targeting the ideas within the practices, was the focus of this chapter. The final consideration, providing the link to learning, is a thread that runs throughout the book.

If you are new to using assessment Probes, we suggest that you try a couple of Probes before returning to review the information in this chapter again after you have some firsthand experience. We also encourage you to visit uncoveringstudentideas.org to share experiences with others who are using Probes in mathematics and science. We look forward to hearing your ideas.

Appendix A

Information on the Standards for Mathematical Practice

The Standards for Mathematical Practice are not a checklist of teacher to-dos but rather support an environment in which the CCSS for mathematics content standards are enacted and are framed by specific expertise that you can use to help students develop their understanding and application of mathematics. (Larson, Lott Adams, Fennell, Dixon, & Kanold, 2012, p. 26)

Formative assessment begins by identifying a learning goal, such as a grade-level expectation from the Common Core State Standards (CCSS). The Common Core State Standards for Mathematics (CCSSM) define what students should understand and be able to do in K–12 mathematics and beyond. Since the grade level expectations in the CCSS define what students should "understand" or "be able to do," it is important for teachers to find out what students know and can do both conceptually or procedurally in relation to the expectation for learning.

In addition to these content standards, an important feature of the CCSSM is the Standards for Mathematical Practices. These practices describe a variety of processes, proficiencies, and dispositions that teachers at all grade levels should seek to develop in their students. Since the CCSSM do not define the methods and strategies used to determine the readiness and prior knowledge necessary to achieve the standards, the mathematics assessment Probes in this book complement CCSSM's eight

Standards for Mathematical Practices and their link to mathematical content (adapted from Keeley & Rose Tobey, 2011, p. 30).

STRUCTURING THE MATHEMATICAL PRACTICE STANDARDS

Figure A.1   The Progression Project's Structure of the Mathematics Standards

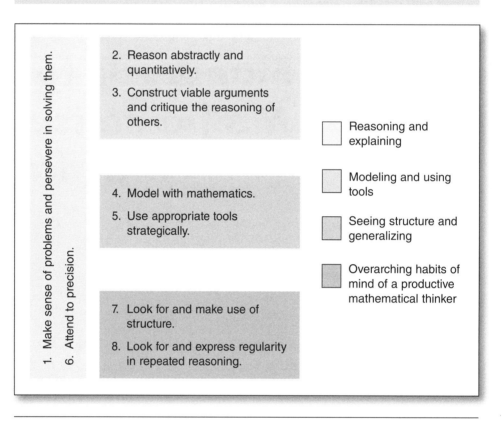

Source: McCallum (2011).

The Institute for Mathematics and Education's Progression Project is organizing the writing of final versions of the progressions documents for the K–12 CCSS. The work is being done by members of the original team along with mathematicians and educators not involved in the initial writing of the standards (Institute for Mathematics and Education, University of Arizona [IME], 2007). The Progression Project created the diagram in Figure A.1 to provide some higher order structure to the practice standards, in the way that the clusters and domains provide higher order structure to the content standards.

The remaining part of this appendix will address each of the practice clusters using language from a variety of resources including the Common Core document (CCSSO, 2010) and the unpacking documents created by North Carolina's Department of Public Instruction (2012a, 2012b, 2012c). Following each of the descriptions of the practices within a cluster, we will describe how the Probes can be used in relationship to the ideas of each cluster. Included in these descriptions are images from practice that high-light various connections.

Reasoning and Explaining Practice Cluster (Practices 2 and 3)

Each of the Probes includes a selected answer response and an explanation prompt. These explanation prompts are the key to the practices within this cluster.

Mathematical Practice 2. Reason abstractly and quantitatively. Students demonstrate proficiency with this practice when they make sense of quantities and relationships while solving tasks. This involves both decontexualizing and contextualizing. When decontextualizing, students need to translate a situation into a numeric or algebraic sentence that models the situation. They represent a wide variety of real world contexts through the use of real numbers and variables in mathematical expressions, equations, and inequalities. When contextualizing, students need to pull from a task information to determine the mathematics required to solve the problem. For example, after a line is fit through data, students interpret the data by interpreting the slope as a rate of change in the context of the problem (CCSSO, 2010; Common Core Standards Writing Team, 2011–2012; North Carolina Department of Public Instruction, 2012a, 2012b, 2012c).

Students who reason abstractly and quantitatively are able to

- move from context to abstraction and back to context;
- make sense of quantities and their relationships in problem situations;
- use quantitative reasoning that includes creating a coherent representation of the problem at hand;
- consider the units involved;
- attend to the meaning of quantities (not just how to compute with them);
- know and flexibly use different properties of operations and objects; and
- use abstract reasoning when measuring and comparing the lengths of objects.

Mathematical Practice 3. Construct viable arguments and critique the reasoning of others. Students demonstrate proficiency with this practice when they accurately use mathematical terms to construct arguments, engage in discussions about problem-solving strategies, examine a variety of problem-solving strategies, and begin to recognize the reasonableness of them, as well as similarities and differences among them. Middle school students should construct arguments using oral or written explanations accompanied by expressions, equations, inequalities, models; and graphs, tables, and other data displays including box plots, dot plots, and histograms (CCSSO, 2010; Common Core Standards Writing Team, 2011–2012; North Carolina Department of Public Instruction, 2012a, 2012b, 2012c).

Students who construct viable arguments and critique the reasoning of others are able to

- make conjectures and build a logical progression of statements to explore the truth of their conjectures;
- recognize and use counterexamples;
- justify their conclusions, communicate them to others, and respond to the arguments of others;
- distinguish correct logic or reasoning from that which is flawed and, if there is a flaw in an argument, explain what it is;
- construct arguments using concrete referents such as objects, drawings, diagrams, and actions; and
- listen or read the arguments of others, decide whether they make sense, and ask useful questions to clarify or improve arguments, including "How did you get that?" "Is that always true?" and "Why does that work?"

Seeing Structure and Generalizing Practice Cluster (Practices 7 and 8)

Young children make sense of their world by looking for patterns and structure and routines. They learn by integrating new information into cognitive structures they have already developed, and they are naturally curious and eager to explore new ideas. Young learners are the perfect candidates for this practice cluster.

Mathematical Practice 7. Look for and make use of structure. Students demonstrate proficiency with this practice when they look for patterns and structures in the number system and other areas of mathematics such as modeling problems involving types of operations. Examples of patterns and structures within the number system include recognition that the commutative property holds for multiplication but not for division, and making use of place value ideas to decompose and recompose numbers in multiple ways. By seeking contextual structures and problem types—including "unknown product," "group size unknown," and "number of groups unknown"—students begin to generalize a model for solving each type of problem (CCSSO, 2010).

Students who look for make use of structure are able to

- notice that 3×4 is the same amount as 4×3 and use this information to simplify more-complex calculations;
- sort a collection of shapes according to their attributes; and
- see things as single objects or as being composed of several objects. (For example, students are able to view the number 10 tenths as the single quantity of 1.)

Mathematical Practice 8. Look for and express regularity in repeated reasoning. Students demonstrate proficiency with this practice when they look for regularity in problem structures when problem solving, notice if calculations are repeated, and look for both general methods and shortcuts. For example, noticing that 2×14 is the same as $2 \times 10 + 2 \times 4$ and that this method can be used to calculate any 1- by 2-digit problem (CCSSO, 2010; North Carolina Department of Public Instruction, 2012b).

Students who look for and express regularity in repeated reasoning are able to

- notice if calculations are repeated;
- look both for general methods and for shortcuts; and
- continually evaluate the reasonableness of their intermediate results.

Modeling and Using Tools Practice Cluster (Practices 4 and 5)

Students use multiple different tools (e.g., rulers, counters, fraction strips, calculators, etc.) in the mathematics classroom. How the tools are used depends on the mathematics topic of focus, and the same tool might be used in a variety of contexts. When given a problem, students need to be able to determine what tool would be appropriate, how the tool could be used in solving the problem, and how to communicate about their process. In the early grades, students often use tools to model a problem. It is also important for students to be able to communicate about the modeling process by representing the process using numbers and symbols.

Mathematical Practice 4. Model with mathematics. Students demonstrate proficiency with this practice when they model real-life mathematical situations with a number sentence or an equation and check to make sure that their equation accurately matches the problem context. Young students often rely on concrete manipulatives and pictorial representations while solving tasks, but the expectation is that they will also write an equation to model problem situations. For example, while solving the story problem, "There are 24 apples arranged in rows. If each row has 8 apples, how many rows of apples are there?," students are expected to write the equation $24 \div 8 = 3$. Likewise, students are expected to create an appropriate problem situation from an equation. For example, students are expected to create a story problem for the equation $\frac{1}{2} + ? = \frac{3}{4}$ such as, "A recipe calls for $\frac{3}{4}$ cup of sugar. How much more sugar do I need if I only have a $\frac{1}{2}$ cup of sugar?" (CCSSO, 2010).

Students who model with mathematics are able to

- apply what they know to make approximations;
- identify important quantities in a problem situation;
- analyze relationships between quantities; and
- reflect on whether the results make sense.

Mathematical Practice 5. Use appropriate tools strategically. Students demonstrate proficiency with this practice when they access and use tools appropriately. These tools may include counters, place value (base-ten) blocks, number lines, and concrete geometric shapes (e.g., three-dimensional solids), and measurement tools (e.g., rulers, scales). Students should also have experiences with educational technologies such as calculators, and virtual manipulatives that support conceptual understanding. During classroom instruction, students should have access to various mathematical tools as well as paper and pencil, and determine which tools are the most appropriate to use. Grade 3–5 students are expected to explain why they used specific mathematical tools. For instance, they may use graph paper or a number line to represent and compare decimals, and protractors to measure angles (CCSSO, 2010; North Carolina Department of Public Instruction, 2012a, 2012b, 2012c).

Students who use appropriate tools strategically are able to

- consider available tools when solving a mathematical problem;
- select tools to match their problem-solving needs;
- explain their choice of a particular tool for a given problem; and
- detect possible errors by reasoning about whether their answer makes sense.

Overarching Habits of Mind of Productive Thinkers Practice Cluster (Practices 1 and 6)

Productive disposition refers to the tendency to see sense in mathematics, to perceive it as both useful and worthwhile, to believe that steady effort in learning mathematics pays off, and to see oneself as an effective learner and doer of mathematics. Developing a productive disposition requires frequent opportunities to make sense of mathematics, to recognize the benefits of perseverance, and to experience the rewards of sense making in mathematics. (NRC, 2001, p. 131)

Mathematical Practice 1. Make sense and persevere in solving problems. Students demonstrate proficiency with this practice when they make sense of the meaning of the task and find an entry point or a way to start the task. Grade 3–5 students also develop a foundation for problem-solving strategies and become independently proficient in using those strategies to solve new tasks. Students use concrete manipulatives and pictorial representations as well as mental mathematics. Students also are expected to persevere while solving tasks; that is, if students reach a point in which they are stuck, they can think about the task in a different way and continue working toward a solution. Mathematically proficient students determine whether their solutions are complete by asking themselves, "Does my answer make sense?" If they determine the answer doesn't make sense, they look for where the error occurred. They listen to the strategies of others, will try different approaches, and will often use another method to check their answers (CCSSO, 2010; North Carolina Department of Public Instruction, 2012a).

Students who use appropriate tools strategically are able to

- start by explaining to themselves the meaning of a problem and looking for entry points to its solution;
- make conjectures about a solution;
- plan a solution pathway rather than simply jumping into a solution attempt;

- monitor and evaluate their progress and change course if necessary;
- use concrete objects or pictures to help conceptualize and solve a problem;
- check their answers to problems using a different method;
- routinely ask themselves, "Does this make sense?"; and
- make sense of the problem-solving approaches of others, noticing similarities and differences among approaches.

Mathematical Practice 6. Attend to precision. Students demonstrate proficiency with this practice when they are precise in their communication, calculations, and measurements. In all mathematical tasks, students in Grades 3–5 should communicate clearly, using grade-level appropriate vocabulary accurately. During tasks involving operating with numbers, students consider whether their answer is reasonable and check their work to ensure the accuracy of solutions. Students state the meaning of the symbols they choose; when measuring or using measurement data, they know that measures must include a number and a unit and are able to specify what unit is appropriate. For instance, they use appropriate labels when creating a line plot (CCSSO, 2010; North Carolina Department of Public Instruction, 2012c).

Students who attend to precision are able to

- use clear definitions in discussion with others and in their own reasoning;
- state the meaning of the symbols they choose, including using the equal sign consistently and appropriately;
- carefully specify units of measurement to clarify their correspondence with quantities in a problem;
- give carefully formulated explanations to other students;
- communicate precisely to others by providing details and/or examples to support their ideas; and
- use informal and formal definitions when sharing their thinking with others.

Chapter 7 covers more about how the Probes support teachers in assessing ideas related to the mathematical practices.

Appendix B

Developing Assessment Probes

Developing an assessment Probe is different from creating appropriate questions for comprehensive diagnostic assessments and summative measures of understanding. The Probes in this book were developed using a process similar to that described in *Mathematics Curriculum Topic Study: Bridging the Gap Between Standards and Practice* (Keeley & Rose, 2006) and the accompanying Leader's Guide (Mundry, Keeley, & Rose Tobey, 2012).

The process is summarized as follows:

- Use national standards to examine concepts and specific ideas related to a topic. The national standards used to develop the Probes for this book are the Common Core State Standards for Mathematics (CCSSO, 2010). The CCSSM define what students should understand and be able to do in K–12 mathematics.

- Within a CCSSM grade-level expectation, select the specific concepts or ideas you plan to address, and identify the relevant research findings. Sources for research findings include the *Research Companion to Principles and Standards for School Mathematics* (NCTM, 2003); *Elementary and Middle School Mathematics: Teaching Developmentally* (Van de Walle et al., 2013), articles from NCTM's *Journal for Research in Mathematics Education* and its *Second Handbook of Research on Mathematics Teaching and Learning* (Lester, 2007a, 2007b), and additional supplemental articles related to the topic.

- Focus on a concept or a specific idea you plan to address with the Probe, and identify the related research findings. Keep the targeted concept small enough to assess with a few items, because Probes are meant to be administered in a short amount of time. Rather than trying to target as much information about a topic as possible, it is better to be more narrow and focused.

- Choose the type of Probe format that lends itself to the situation. (See more information on Probe format in Chapter 1's "What Is the Structure of a Probe?".) Develop the stem (the prompt), key (correct response), and distractors (incorrect responses derived from research findings) that match the developmental level of your students.
- Share your assessment Probe(s) with colleagues for constructive feedback, pilot with students, and modify as needed.

Feedback on the assessment Probes developed for this resource was collected from Grades 3–5 educators across multiple states, and the Probes were piloted with students across multiple grade levels. The feedback and student work were used to revise the Probes and to support the development of the accompanying Teacher Notes.

Appendix C

Action Research Reflection Template

QUEST Cycle

Questions to Consider About the **Key Mathematical Concepts**

What is the concept you wish to target? Is the concept at grade level or is it a prerequisite?

Uncovering Student Understanding **About the Key Concepts**

How will you collect information from students (e.g., paper pencil, interview, student response system, etc.)? What form will you use (e.g., one-page Probe, card sort, etc.)? Are there adaptations you plan to make? Review the summary of typical student responses.

Exploring Excerpts From Educational Resources and Related Research

Review the quotes from research about common difficulties related to the Probe. What do you predict to be common understandings and/or misunderstandings for your students?

Surveying the Prompts and Selected Responses in the Probe

Sort by selected responses then re-sort by trends in thinking. What common understandings/misunderstandings did the Probe elicit? How do these elicited understandings/misunderstandings compare to those listed in the Teacher Notes?

Teaching Implications and Considerations

Review the bulleted list and decide how you will take action. What actions did you take? How did you assess the impact of those actions? What are your next steps?

References

Ashlock, R. B. (2006). *Error patterns in computation.* Upper Saddle River, NJ: Pearson.

Askew, M., & Wiliam, D. (1995). *Recent research in mathematics education 5–16.* London, UK: HMSO.

Bamberger, H., Oberdorf, C., & Schulz-Farrell, K. (2010). *Math misconceptions: From misunderstanding to deep understanding.* Portsmouth, NH: Heinemann.

Battista, M. T. (2002). Learning in an inquiry-based classroom: Fifth graders' enumeration of cubes in 3D arrays. In J. Sowder & B. Schappelle (Eds.), *Lessons learned from research* (pp. 75–84). Reston, VA: National Council of Teachers of Mathematics.

Bay Area Mathematics Task Force. (1999). *A mathematics sourcebook for elementary and middle school teachers.* Novato, CA: Arena Press.

Black, B., & Harrison, C. (2004). *Science inside the black box: Assessment for learning in the science classroom.* London: NFER/Nelson.

Black, P., Harrison C., Lee, C., Marshall, B., & Wiliam, D. (2004). Working inside the black box: Assessment for learning in the classroom. *Phi Delta Kappan, 86*(1), 8–21.

Burns, M. (2005). Looking at how students reason. *Educational Leadership: Assessment to Promote Learning, 63*(3), 26–31.

Common Core Standards Writing Team. (2011a). *Progressions for the Common Core State Standards in Mathematics (draft): K–5, number and operations in base ten.* Retrieved from http://ime.math.arizona.edu/progressions/#products

Common Core Standards Writing Team. (2011b). *Progressions for the Common Core State Standards in Mathematics (draft): K–5, number and operations—fractions.* Retrieved from http://ime.math.arizona.edu/progressions/#products

Common Core Standards Writing Team. (2011c). *Progressions for the Common Core State Standards in Mathematics (draft): K–5, operations and algebraic thinking.* Retrieved from http://ime.math.arizona.edu/progressions/#products

Common Core Standards Writing Team. (2012a). *Progressions for the Common* Core Standards Writing Team *(draft): K–5, geometric measurement.* Retrieved from http://ime.math.arizona.edu/progressions/#products

Common Core Standards Writing Team. (2012b). *Progressions for the Common Core State Standards in Mathematics (draft): K–6, geometry.* Retrieved from http://ime.math.arizona.edu/progressions/#products

Council of Chief State School Officers (CCSSO). (2008). *Attributes of effective formative assessment.* Retrieved from http://www.ccsso.org/Resources/Publications/Attributes_of_Effective_Formative_Assessment.html

Council of Chief State School Officers (CCSSO). (2010). *Common core state standards.* Retrieved from http://corestandards.org

Cramer, K. A., Post, T. R., & del Mas, R. C. (2002). Initial fraction learning by fourth- and fifth-grade students: A comparison of the effects of using commercial curricula with the effects of using the rational number project curriculum. *Journal for Research in Mathematics Education, 33*(2), 111–144.

DuFour, R., DuFour, R, Eaker, R., & Many, T. (2006). *Learning by doing: A handbook for professional learning communities at work.* Bloomington, IN: Solution Tree.

Fosnot, C., & Dolk, M. (2001). *Young mathematicians at work: Constructing number sense, addition, and subtraction.* Portsmouth, NH: Heinemann.

Fuchs, L. S., Fuchs, D., Prentice, K., Burch, M., Hamlett, C. L., Owen, R., . . . Jancek, D. (2003). Explicitly teaching for transfer: Effects on third-grade students' mathematical problem solving. *Journal of Educational Psychology, 95,* 293–305.

Fuys, D. J., & A. K. Liebov. Geometry and spatial sense. In *Research Ideas for the Classroom,* edited by R. J. Jensen, 219. New York: Macmillan, 1993.

Garcia, L. (2012). *How to get students talking! Generating math talk that supports math learning.* Retrieved from http://www.mathsolutions.com/documents/How_to_Get_Students_Talking.pdf

Hartweg, K. (2011). Representations and rafts. *Mathematics Teaching in the Middle School, 17*(1), 40–47.

Heritage, M. (2010). *Formative assessment: Making it happen in the classroom.* Thousand Oaks, CA: Corwin.

Hiebert, J. (2002). Decimal fractions. In Chambers, D. L., & National Council of Teachers of Mathematics, I. A. (2002). *Putting research into practice in the elementary grades: Readings from journals of the National Council of Teachers of Mathematics* (119–120). Madison: Wisconsin Center for Education Research, University of Wisconsin-Madison.

Institute for Mathematics and Education, University of Arizona (IME). (2007). *Progressions documents for the common core math standards: About this project.* Retrieved from http://math.arizona.edu/~ime/progressions/

Keeley, P. (2012, April). Misunderstanding misconceptions. *Science Scope, 35*(8), 12–13.

Keeley, P., & Rose, C. (2006). *Mathematics curriculum topic study: Bridging the gap between standards and practice.* Thousand Oaks, CA: Corwin.

Keeley, P., & Rose Tobey, C. (2011). *Mathematics formative assessment: 75 practical strategies for linking assessment, instruction and learning.* Thousand Oaks, CA: Corwin.

Kurz, T., & Garcia, J. (2012). Moving beyond factor trees. *Mathematics Teaching in the Middle School, 18*(1), 52–60.

Larson, M., Lott Adams, T., Fennell, F., Dixon, K., & Kanold, T. (2012). *Common Core Mathematics in a PLC at work: Grades K–2.* Bloomington, IN: Solution Tree.

Lester, F. K. Jr. (Ed). (2007a). *Second handbook of research on mathematics teaching and learning:* A project of the National Council of Teachers of Mathematics, vol. 1. Charlotte, NC: Information Age Publishing.

Lester, F. K. Jr. (Ed). (2007b). *Second handbook of research on mathematics teaching and learning:* A project of the National Council of Teachers of Mathematics, vol. 2. Charlotte, NC: Information Age Publishing.

Loucks-Horsley, S., Love, N., Stiles, K., Mundry, S., & Hewson, P. (2003). *Designing professional development for teachers of science and mathematics.* Thousand Oaks, CA: Corwin.

Mack, N. K. (2007). Gaining insights into children's geometric knowledge. *Teaching Children Mathematics, 14*(4), 238–245.

Martinie, S. L. (2007). Middle school rational number knowledge. *Dissertation Abstracts International Section A,* 68.

McCallum, B. (2011, March 10). Structuring the mathematical practices [Web log post]. Retrieved from http://commoncoretools.me/2011/03/10/structuring-the-mathematical-practices/

McTighe, J., & O'Conner, K. (2005). Seven practices for effective learning. *Educational Leadership: Assessment to Promote Learning, 63*(3), 10–17.

Mestre, J. (1989). *Hispanic and Anglo students' misconceptions in mathematics.* Charleston, WV: Appalachia Educational Laboratory. Retrieved from ERIC database (ED313192).

Minton, L. (2007). *What if your ABCs were your 123s? Building connections between literacy and numeracy.* Thousand Oaks, CA: Corwin.

Moss, C., & Brookhart, S. (2012). *Learning targets: Helping students aim for understanding in today's lesson.* Alexandria, VA: ASCD.

Mundry, S., Keeley, P., & Rose Tobey, C. (2012). *Facilitator's guide to mathematics curriculum topic study.* Thousand Oaks, CA: Corwin.

Munier, V. Devichi, C. & Merle, H. (2008). A physical situation as a way to teach angle. *Teaching Children Mathematics, 14*(7), 402–407.

National Council of Teachers of Mathematics (NCTM). (1993). *Research ideas for the classroom: Middle grades mathematics.* New York: MacMillan.

National Council of Teachers of Mathematics (NCTM). (2000). *Principles and standards for school mathematics.* Reston, VA: Author.

National Council of Teachers of Mathematics (NCTM). (2003). *Research companion to principles and standards for school mathematics.* Reston, VA: Author.

National Research Council (NRC). (2001). *Adding it up: Helping children learn mathematics.* Washington, DC: National Academies Press.

National Research Council (NRC). (2005). *How students learn mathematics in the classroom.* Washington, DC: National Academies Press.

Naylor, S., & Keogh, B. (2000). *Concept cartoons in science education.* Sandbach, UK: Millgate House Education.

North Carolina Department of Public Instruction. (2012a). Instructional support tools for achieving new standards: K grade mathematics unpacked content. Retrieved from http://www.ncpublicschools.org/acre/standards/common-core-tools/#unmath

North Carolina Department of Public Instruction. (2012b). Instructional support tools for achieving new standards: 1st grade mathematics unpacked content. Retrieved from http://www.ncpublicschools.org/acre/standards/common-core-tools/#unmath

North Carolina Department of Public Instruction. (2012c). Instructional support tools for achieving new standards: 2nd grade mathematics unpacked content. Retrieved from http://www.ncpublicschools.org/acre/standards/common-core-tools/#unmath

Resnick, L. (1983). Mathematics and science learning: A new conception. *Science, 220,* 477–478.

Rose, C., & Arline, C. (2009). *Uncovering student thinking in mathematics, grades 6–12: 30 formative assessment probes for the secondary classroom.* Thousand Oaks, CA: Corwin.

Rose, C., Minton, L., & Arline, C. (2007). *Uncovering student thinking in mathematics: 25 formative assessment probes.* Thousand Oaks, CA: Corwin.

Rose Tobey, C. & Minton, L. (2011). *Uncovering student thinking in mathematics grades K–5: 25 formative assessment probes for the elementary classroom.* Thousand Oaks, CA: Corwin.

Ross, S. (2002). Place value: Problem solving and written assessment. *Teaching Children Mathematics*, 8(7), 419–423.

Rubenstein, R., & Thompson, D. (2006). Understanding and supporting children's mathematical vocabulary development. *Teaching Children Mathematics, 9*(2), 107–112.

Ryan, J., & Williams, J. (2007). *Children's mathematics 4–15.* Berkshire, UK: Open University Press.

Siebert, D., & Gaskin, N. (2006). Creating, naming, and justifying fractions. *Teaching Children Mathematics, 12*(8), 394–400.

Siegler, R., Carpenter, T., Fennell, F., Geary, D., Lewis, J., Okamoto, Y., Thompson, L., & Wray, J. (2010). *Developing effective fractions instruction for kindergarten through 8th grade: A practice guide* (NCEE #2010–4039). Washington, DC: National Center for Education Evaluation and Regional Assistance, Institute of Education Sciences, U.S. Department of Education. Retrieved from whatworks.ed.gov/publications/practiceguides.

Small, M. (2009). *Good questions: Great ways to differentiate mathematics instruction.* New York: Teachers College Press.

Sowder, J. (2002). Place value as the key to teaching decimal operations. In Chambers, D. L., & National Council of Teachers of Mathematics, I. A. (2002). *Putting research into practice in the elementary grades: Readings from journals of the National Council of Teachers of Mathematics* (113–118). Madison: Wisconsin Center for Education Research, University of Wisconsin-Madison.

Stepans, J. I., Schmidt, D. L., Welsh, K. M., Reins, K. J., & Saigo, B. W. (2005). *Teaching for K–12 mathematical understanding using the conceptual change model.* St. Cloud, MN: Saiwood.

Tobey, C. R., & Fagan, E. R. (2013). *Uncovering student thinking about mathematics in the common core, grades K–2: 20 formative assessments.* Thousand Oaks, CA: Corwin.

Van de Walle, J. A. (2007). *Elementary and middle school mathematics* (6th ed.). Boston, MA: Pearson.

Van de Walle, J. A., Karp, K., & Bay-Williams, J. (2013). *Elementary and middle school mathematics* (8th ed.). Boston, MA: Pearson.

Watson, B., & Konicek, R. (1990). Teaching for conceptual change: Confronting children's experience. *Phi Delta Kappan, 71*(9), 680–684.

Wiliam, D. (2011). *Embedded formative assessment.* Bloomington, IN: Solution Tree.

Wylie, E., Gullickson, A. R., Cummings, K. E., Egelson, P. E., Noakes, L. A., Norman, K. M., & Veeder, S. A. (2012). *Improving formative assessment practice to empower student learning.* Thousand Oaks, CA: Corwin.

Xin, Y. (2008). The effect of schema-based instruction in solving mathematics word problems: An emphasis on prealgebraic conceptualization of multiplicative relations. *Journal for Research in Mathematics Education, 39*(5), 526–551.

Yetkin, E. (2003). *Student difficulties in learning elementary mathematics.* ERIC Clearinghouse for Science Mathematics and Environmental Education. (Document Reproduction Service No. Retrieved from ERIC database (ED482727).

Zazkis, R., & Liljedahl, P. (2004). Understanding primes: The role of representation. *Journal for Research in Mathematics Education, 35*(3), 164–186.

Index

CORWIN

A SAGE Company

The Corwin logo—a raven striding across an open book—represents the union of courage and learning. Corwin is committed to improving education for all learners by publishing books and other professional development resources for those serving the field of PreK–12 education. By providing practical, hands-on materials, Corwin continues to carry out the promise of its motto: **"Helping Educators Do Their Work Better."**